THE GREAT AMERICAN FAMILY

A Story of Political Disenchantment

WEAM NAMOU

HERMiZ
PUBLiSHING
Copyright © 2016 by Weam Namou

Library of Congress Cataloging-in-Publication Data:
2 0 1 6 9 0 6 4 6 9

Namou, Weam

The Great American Family
A Story of Political Disenchantment
(creative nonfiction)

ISBN 978-0-9776790-5-8 (paperback)
First Edition

Published in the United States of America by:
Hermiz Publishing, Inc.
Sterling Heights, MI

10 9 8 7 6 5 4 3 2 1

Contents

To the families who have suffered unnecessarily by unjust laws

INTRODUCTION

In 2010, a family approached me to write a story about their daughter, Dawn Hanna. At the time, Dawn was serving a six-year prison sentence for conspiring to sell telecom equipment to Iraq during the sanctions. After her trial, her so-called co-conspirator revealed that he was a CIA operative and that Dawn, in fact, was innocent. He said that she did not know the equipment was going to Iraq because it was a top-secret operation intended to allow authorities to listen in on Saddam and his men. The court ignored this new information and forced Dawn to report to prison.

I initially did not want to write this story because it was political, and I was tired, often even afraid of, politics, especially when it dealt with Iraq. Yet I came from a country where creativity and responsibility oftentimes went hand-in-hand, from a society which dates back to Prophet Abraham's traditional and tribal ways, where people do not act as individuals but as members of a larger group. The Dawn Hanna case had a humanitarian element that I could not ignore. It was about government abuse, the sanctions, and the post-9/11 sensationalism in the US against the Arab American community.

I was a child when my family and I fled Iraq over thirty years ago because of Iraq's totalitarian government. Today, as a mother, I want my children to grow up in the great nation my family risked their lives to come to for freedom. I felt it was my responsibility to write this story because, among other things, I did not want my children to ever have to endure in the United States the same political climate my parents endured in Iraq.

CHAPTER 1
The Dawn Hanna Case

It was a warm afternoon in May of 2010, and the last thing I wanted to do was attend the lunch meeting Bonnie set up with a few Iraqi American businessmen regarding an Iraqi American project I was working on. The war with Iraq was in its seventh year. As an Iraqi American journalist, novelist, and amateur filmmaker, I mostly wrote about the Iraqi American experience, and frankly, I was tired of Iraq this and Iraq that. I wanted to pick up the subject of Iraq with my fingers and toss it with the rest of the laundry into the washing machine so that all the filth it had picked up in the twentieth century would be wrung out. The unsoiled and colorful threads of that land and culture would therefore reappear and glisten like a diamond under the sun, allowing me to write from a place of love, not sorrow.

Maybe, by some mysterious divine intervention, this meeting would be cancelled. Then I would be able to stay home with my children and finish cooking and doing house-work while watching *The Real Housewives of New Jersey*, the reality show I tuned to the way men tuned to sports. Now that I was married and had an eleven-month-old son and a four-year-old daughter, I could barely travel to the produce market to buy lettuce and tomatoes, let alone sit at a lunch meeting with people who had not yet healed from the op-pressions their birth country had bestowed upon them. As a result, they tended to discuss their stories as if they were sitting at a therapists' office rather than focus on the work at hand.

If I had any brains, I would've canceled the meeting my-self instead of waiting for God to do it, then put on my gym shoes and take a long walk down my usual path, where I'd eventually reach a house with two baby pear trees standing side by side, like sisters. One had green pears and the other had red pears. The trees were always abundant and close to the sidewalk, welcoming a stranger's hand. On these walks, I usually plucked a red pear, rubbed it with my hands, and ate it. A few feet from the house with the pear trees was a high-fenced house. Branches filled with baby green plums fell over the fence, like the hair of Rapunzel. I sometimes plucked a few of those as well.

Between putting on my makeup and getting dressed for the lunch meeting, I handed my daughter a bowl of cereal, refilled my son's sippy cup with milk, and made sure the rice on the stove did not burn and the pot of green beans did not over boil. I imagined the meeting getting canceled even as I pulled out of the driveway and headed to Sahara restaurant, an Iraqi restaurant a few miles south of my house.

The others were already there. One of the men at the meeting happened to be my brother's long-time friend, Steve, who I walked down the aisle with at my brother's wedding twenty years ago. There were two other men I had never met, a Louie and his business partner. And there was Bonnie, the woman who'd set up this meeting. All were Iraqi-born and had shortened or changed their name so Americans could easily pronounce it. When I first arrived to the United States, I'd tried on different names like Amanda, Amy, and Wendy, but none fit quite right, so I stuck with the one my parents gave me.

"What a small world!" Steve said. "When Bonnie mentioned your name, I thought, 'It has to be the same Weam I know.' There are not that many people with that name."

Steve was the only one wearing a suit. The other two men were in casual pants and shirts. Bonnie, who claimed she was a model but had no portfolio, though she did look like a model, was in high heels and a stylish skirt. A designer handbag was on the floor beside her feet.

"So Weam, I hear you're a journalist and you write books," Steve said. "What kind of books do you write?"

"I write true life stories about the Iraqi American experience."

"That's great. Few people here realize how rich Iraq's history and people are."

"Why don't you write history books?" Louie asked. "Americans know nothing about us. Before the 2003 war, it's like they had never heard of Iraq. Iraq is ancient Mesopotamia, the cradle of civilization. It dates back over five thousand years."

"Actually, over seven thousand years," I said. I shared with them the story of how, before 2003, people who asked me where I was from repeatedly confused Iraq with Iran, even after I corrected them.

"When did you come to America?" Steve asked.

"In February 1981."

"Just a few weeks before the end of the Iran hostage crisis, that's why. If a country receives media coverage, people learn about it. Otherwise, forget it."

"Iraq had coverage in 1991 when America bombed it for forty-three days in a row," I said.

The waitress delivered a combination platter of kabobs and shawarmas, the preferred route with large group parties at Middle Eastern restaurants. Like in biblical times, the tray of food is placed in the center for everyone to share. Jesus spoke of this when he said, "One who dips his bread in the dish with me will betray me," and Prophet Muhammad encouraged it by saying, "Eat together and not separately, for the blessing is associated with the company."

When the food made its debut, it allowed for the topic of politics to slip off the table as if it were a mere crumb. With Iraqis or Middle Easterners in general, conversations often gravitate to politics. None of us really like this subject, but we can't help it. It is in our DNA. We were born in Iraq, a country habitually involved in war. Most of us came to the United States when Iraq and the United States were heavily courting. Many think they had even eloped. This secret marriage did not last, and before long, ended in divorce. The problem was that no matter how ugly their fights and divorce, their relationship was never really going to be over, given the bond they once had and the lifelong oil contracts they'd signed together. As their product, their children, we could not sever our political ties, which was the base of their marriage.

"Weam, who was the most interesting person you've ever interviewed?" Steve asked.

I had to think for a minute. "I once visited Ray, the lord of the so-called 'Chaldean mafia.' He's in a Detroit prison. We met two or three times, and you know what the first thing he said to me was? 'We were not a mafia; we were just kids in pursuit of happiness. We were poor. Our families were poor. And we wanted to make money.' He was, like, seventeen years old when he was indicted, and the government and media sensationalized his case by adding that word – mafia."

"You visited Ray?" Steve asked, pouring northern bean stew over his rice.

"Yes." I remembered Ray telling me about the one and only memory he had of his childhood in Iraq. He was a year and a half when his mother gave him a peach. When he ate it, juice dripped from his mouth. His mother became angry because it was Easter and he was dressed in his new clothes.

"I heard he's appealing," Steve said.

"That's what I heard too. I guess the prosecutors made a deal with this guy to testify against Ray. The guy who testified ended up getting probation and Ray got life in prison."

"Well, the government has the right to make deals with witnesses."

"They do, but the jury must know about it because it might change the weight of the witness statement. Prosecutors are supposed to share all evidence with the defense in order to have a fair trial."

"Have you ever heard of Dawn Hanna?" Louie asked with a particularly serious expression.

"No, I haven't," I said.

"She was all over the news last year."

"I try to avoid the news. If it were up to me, I would have all the Arabic news channels that my husband watches removed from our satellite TV and replaced with the *Real Housewives* series, the *Atlanta* and the *New Jersey Housewives* being my two favorites."

They all laughed.

"Yes, that is what I love – marriage and family, no matter how wacky and dysfunctional, as long as there is no killing involved."

"You need to meet Dawn," Louie said. "You really do. She's an incredible person and has one hell of a story. I've known her and her family forever, and the two of you seem to have much in common. She's about your age – in her late thirties – and has traveled the world and met with higher-ups like prime ministers and multi-millionaires. She's smart, generous and…" He became dismayed. "…was very successful."

"Is she Chaldean?"

"Her father is. He was born in Iraq. Her mother is American."

"Where does she live?"

"She lived close by, in Rochester Hills. Now she's in a federal prison in Kentucky."

"For what?"

"She sold telecommunication equipment to someone who told her that the equipment was going to Turkey when really he was sending it to Iraq. This was before the 2003 war, when Iraq was under sanctions and it was illegal for Americans to do business with Iraq. After she was sentenced, she found out that the guy she was working with was actually a CIA agent. The CIA stuff was never mentioned during the trial."

"How did she find out he was a CIA agent?"

"It's a long and complicated story. You can talk to her over the phone."

I nodded, wondering how I could wiggle away from this request. Earlier today, as I pulled out of my driveway, I had taken a long look at my suburban home and decided that this was the last time I would attend a business meeting. I wanted to stay home, raise my young children, and write something that was big and important. I wanted my writing to have the same effect as a nurse, a doctor, an attorney or a police officer, professions that are not solely self-indulgent but save and change lives.

"You can also request permission to visit her in prison, in Kentucky," he said. "It's only a seven-hour drive."

Only? I thought, pouring potato curry over the saffron rice. *This guy was nuts!* It was difficult enough finding someone to watch my children for a two-hour lunch meeting, let alone for a whole day's trip. And of course, my husband would be *entirely* supportive of me going to some far away prison to visit a woman I'd never met before, a criminal at that.

"Her family is looking for someone to write a book about her story," he said.

I almost choked on my coffee.

"Are you okay?" Bonnie asked.

"Yes," I said, patting my lips with a napkin.

People often assume they have a story I should write, a bestseller and an Oscar winner. I do not try to explain that having a great story and writing a great story are two separate things, especially when you have small children wedging themselves between you and the computer while Barney's songs or SpongeBob's laughter and disputes over the crabby patty play loudly in the background.

"Weam, Dawn was an all-American girl and she was railroaded," he said, evidently sensing my discomfort. As we continued with our lunch, he went on to tell me how Dawn's mother raised her to have great American values. She put her in Girl Scout Brownies, and Dawn earned badges for a whole lot of activities. She played baseball, soccer, and ice skated. When Dawn was seventeen, she got a full-ride scholarship in the honors program at the University of Detroit Mercy, a private Catholic university. She decided to be a lawyer, and in just three years, she received an associate degree in paralegal studies and a bachelor's degree in legal administration despite working full-time and traveling overseas through an international program. She studied at Oxford in England, at Beijing Institute of Technology in China, and also at Shanghai. She did her internship at the 52nd District Court in Rochester Hills, but after taking the LSAT, she changed her major and instead got a master's degree in international business and marketing management. Man, Dawn had everything going for her, and then the government came along and messed her all up."

He took a slice of pita bread and passed the basket to Bonnie. In return, Bonnie handed him the plate of pickled vegetables. They eyed each other. Bonnie was a flirtatious woman who used her sex appeal to get involved in other people's deals. And she was, to put it kindly, not all there. She was often visited by the Virgin Mary, she told me, and she had close connections with Angelina Jolie and the whole government of Iraq.

"They even tried to put her brother Darrin in prison," Louie said, "but thank God, the jury found him innocent. Otherwise, that whole family would be wiped out by grief right now."

I was curious why her brother was found innocent. As if reading my thoughts, Louie said, "Darrin is a genius!"

I raised my eyebrows, beginning to question how genuine his descriptions were.

"I'm not kidding. That's his nickname." He turned toward Steve and pointed at me, laughing. "She doesn't believe me!" He looked at me again. "They call him a genius because he's like a little Einstein. This guy started his own computer company when he was seventeen years old. He got millions of dollars to do science work, like finding safe places for people to go to before a hurricane hits."

The waitress brought us each a glass of cardamom tea.

"What's her last name again?"

"Hanna, but they're known as the Shemami's."

I frowned. "The Shemami's? Is she related to Raad Shemami?"

"That's her uncle, her dad's brother. You know him?"

"He chaperoned me to Iraq ten years ago," I said, thinking of the trip I'd made to Iraq, most of which I had since blocked out of my memory.

"So Weam, can I set up a meeting with you and her family?"

"Yes," I said halfheartedly. I noticed Bonnie wink at Louie.

The image of Maysoon flashed before my eyes, and I thought, *that's who Bonnie reminds me of!* Raad had also chaperoned Maysoon and her mother to Iraq during my trip.

Although Bonnie was much older and prettier than Maysoon, they had similar personalities. They said the wrong things at the wrong time, and no matter how much one tried to explain a situation to them, their perception of it was botched up. The difference was that, unlike Maysoon, Bonnie had no chaperone or mother to prevent her from utilizing her not-all-there self. Knowing this, I had warned Bonnie ahead of time not to say more than a few words at the meetings we attended together.

On my drive home, I kept thinking of my trip to Iraq. Those three and a half weeks had exhausted me physically, mentally, emotionally, and spiritually, so much so that the day I returned home and went back to work, I had woken up in one of the aisles of the video store I managed. A customer was kneeling beside me. He asked, "Are you okay?"

"Yes," I said, slowly getting up and looking around me in confusion.

CHAPTER 2
My Trip to Iraq

The van was pitch black inside, the windows covered by a thick substance that, given the time and place, could not be snow. We were traveling the desert en route to Baghdad in the middle of the night, in the month of April. I had lived in Michigan for twenty years and knew what snow was, and this was not it. This substance wasn't the type to melt under the sun or be removed by windshield wipers, but rather, it resembled drapery, heaps of heavy drapery. It caused our van to go five miles an hour and our driver to see only an inch or two of the road ahead of him, even though he focused his stare out the windshield. Whatever this was, I had not seen it when it first accumulated because I had fallen asleep.

"What is this?" I asked our chaperone, Raad, who was in his sixties and now more visible as my eyes became accustomed to the darkness.

"It's a sandstorm." He grinned, as if his experiences with

sandstorms were as natural as eating a cup of yogurt. "Sandstorms are ten times worse than snowstorms. In a sandstorm, you can barely see, move, or breathe."

"Why doesn't the driver turn on the defrost button?" asked Maysoon, another passenger who was heading to Baghdad. Not counting the driver, the van carried four passengers: Maysoon and I, born as Christians in Iraq, raised in the US; Maysoon's mother, Victoria; and our chaperone, Raad, who frowned every time Maysoon opened her mouth.

"Can't we stop somewhere until the storm ends?" I asked.

Turning his attention away from Maysoon without answering her question, Raad's natural grin returned. "Are you kidding? We'll get robbed by bandits."

My heart pounded. We were in the middle of a forlorn highway, engulfed by a sandstorm, and even though the year was 2000, there were no mobile or pay phones to dial for help.

"How much money are you carrying?" Raad asked.

"Three thousand dollars." I did not tell him it was in a pouch my oldest sister stitched to my bra because the women in the family agreed that Iraqi robbers would not stoop so low as to look there. "It's gift money. I only brought three hundred dollars for myself as spending money."

Three hundred dollars in Iraq during the UN-imposed sanctions was a whole lot of money. An entire family could live off fifty dollars per month.

"Let me give you some advice," he said. "No matter what happens, how much your relatives beg and tell you sob stories, make sure that after you give them their gift money, you do not give up those three hundred dollars that you brought for yourself. Do you understand?"

That's exactly what my mother had advised.

"In Iraq, credit cards and checkbooks are more useless than a rock," he said. "Outside of Iraq, the Iraqi dinar is less useful than toilet paper. So if you're in a jam, where are you going to get money from? Dig it from under the ground?"

I nodded, and he glanced at me with amusement. I didn't know what was going through his head, but I suspected it was similar to what my mother thought; visiting Iraq when it was under sanctions was insane. My mother had strongly advised me to postpone this trip until conditions in Iraq got better, as if that were imaginable. I took her advice for years, one eye on the clock, the other on the news, and Iraq never saw rest. So I spent year after year visiting different parts of the world, but not my birth country. Had my father been alive, he would have given me his blessings to go.

What my mother couldn't understand was that I missed Iraq, badly. I had a wonderful childhood there and *poof!*, it was all gone. One day, I opened my eyes and I was in Jordan with my family, living in an apartment and awaiting a visa for the United States. I have no recollection of our actual departure. Everything happened so fast and in secrecy because we couldn't let anyone know we were heading for America. No one told me or my younger brother what our family was up to, and so we didn't get a chance to say goodbye to our friends or neighbors – just a few of our close family members, which again I have no recollection of doing. We disappeared as quickly as sugar in a cup of hot tea, and then we began a new life.

A few had prophesied that the world would end in the

year 2000, and I figured if I ever wanted to see my birthplace again and squelch this nostalgia, I had to do it early that year to avoid separation from my home in Michigan during the apocalypse. Furthermore, I only had two elderly aunts left in Iraq. If they died, my mother would more firmly be able to deny my going on this trip because in Iraq, I would have to stay at a close relative's home, not a hotel. This was Baghdad, not Hawaii.

The sandstorm ended, and I could once again stare out the window. There was nothing to see except various large delivery trucks, some packed to the brim with ropes, lined up for miles on the side of the road. I asked Raad what they were for.

"People smuggling things into Iraq," he said.

"I thought Iraq was under sanctions."

"It is, but that hasn't stopped other countries from dealing with it. How else would it have survived?"

Jordanians, Saudis, Egyptians, Russians, and the Chinese all made money out of Iraq during the sanctions. Before the sanctions, Iraq had imported about 70 percent of its food, medicine, and chemicals for agriculture. Without international trade, it was not able to feed itself despite its wealth of oil reserves. Saddam found a temporary solution. He gathered the smugglers and cut a deal with them. Prior to this deal, these smugglers smuggled out of Iraq things like sheep cattle and palm dates, as they were known to be the tastiest in the Middle East, to neighboring countries like Saudi Arabia and Israel. They smuggled into Iraq such illegal items as handguns, bullets, or drugs from Turkey, Iran, or Afghanistan. If caught, the Iraqi government confiscated the items and fined or sentenced the smuggler, depending on the crime – except in the case of drugs like heroin or cocaine, which was an automatic death penalty. The Iraqi government, along with many other Arab governments, was intolerant, and still is intolerant, of drugs entering the country.

At this gathering of professional smugglers, Saddam gave the men the green light to do business as smugglers, but there was a catch. They could smuggle out of the country whatever they wanted, but they had to smuggle into the country whatever the Iraqi government wanted. So someone could take oil out of Iraq, for instance, and in exchange bring in car tires. Another could take whiskey out of Iraq and into Saudi Arabia. There was an abundance of liquor factories in Iraq and the cost of each bottle was next to nothing, but in Saudi Arabia, it was prohibited and sold for $200. The punishment for being caught drinking alcohol in Saudi Arabia is a jail term and public lashing.

In return, the smuggler would bring into Iraq US dollars, which Saddam would use to buy wheat, fertilizer, and tractors from Jordan or Syria. Or a smuggler brought in seeds, wood, cement, and construction material. Smuggling negotiation was one of the methods Saddam used to keep the country from dying. With money and equipment, he could keep farming alive. He also encouraged farmers by buying wheat from them at a much higher cost than the regular price so they would not leave farming and go into other professions.

It was daylight and we stopped at a rest area, which had a small restaurant and a grocery store, to eat lunch. Maysoon looked with disgust at the restaurant we sat in and refused to eat the chicken and rice the waiter served. Raad insisted she eat something because we had a long journey ahead of us.

"I don't eat when I travel," she said.

"You're staying in Baghdad for two months," he said. "You won't eat that whole time?"

"No." She even refused to touch the tea, leaving the restaurant with a sour face.

Maysoon was a tall and husky girl, so I didn't know how she would survive in Iraq. According to my mother, some of the homes in Iraq did not have toilets, but that couldn't be right. In the city of Ur, the birthplace of Prophet Abraham which is mentioned several times in the Bible as Ur of the Chaldees (referring to the Chaldeans, my ancestors, who settled in the area about 900 BC), toilets were developed dating back to around 2000 BC.

Now that we'd experienced the turn of the twenty-first century, surely every home had a standard squat toilet, a hole in the ground, the kinds used by royalty in medieval castles which required the squat posture that is popular and encouraged in yoga classes and weight training. Some homes were likely to even have modern toilets. Twenty years ago, my sister's bathroom had a modern toilet and beside it a bidet, which allowed for a type of a sink that is a few centuries old and is popular around the world – except in North America – because it is considered more sanitary and environment-friendly.

Our next stop was a little marketplace where Raad advised us to buy cheese, Nido milk powder, eggs, and soap for relatives. Those items were very expensive, lacking, or diluted in Baghdad because of the sanctions.

"Give them this and buy groceries for the homes you'll be staying in and you'll be treated like queens," he said.

As we neared the Iraqi border, Maysoon suddenly grew frantic over the idea of custom agents finding menstrual pads amongst her belongings. Her mother, embarrassed, tried to shut her up, but to no avail. Then Maysoon's face turned happy. "Wait a second," she said. "These people don't know what menstrual pads look like, do they?"

"Are you stupid? Of course they do."

"I doubt it, Mom. They're not that advanced."

What amazed me more than Maysoon's high-and-mighty attitude and her ignorance was my mother's awareness early on of Maysoon's qualities.

At Detroit Metro Airport, my overly worried mother was put at ease when she saw that Victoria and her daughter were part of our small group. It turned out that my mom and Victoria had been neighbors in Baghdad some thirty odd years ago. The two sat and chatted for a while; this was before 9/11, when family and friends could hang out with the passengers at Detroit Metro Airport before they got on the plane. I heard Victoria assuring my mother that she would look after me, a twenty-nine year-old woman, as if I was her own daughter. My mother thanked and blessed her profusely.

"You don't know how happy I am that Victoria is coming along," my mother said to me. "She is an educated and smart woman." She glanced toward Maysoon, who sat on the window edge, looking out the window at the airplane next to our gate. "Quite the opposite of her daughter."

"How do you know?" I asked.

My mother hadn't even exchanged one word with Maysoon.

"You can tell from her appearance and…well, the way she is gazing through the window at the airplane."

I couldn't understand how that was enough proof, but it turned out to be true. From the very beginning, Maysoon acted as though the Middle East was too primitive for her when she'd left Iraq a mere ten years prior, at age nineteen. During our drive from Amman airport to the Sheraton hotel, where we spent the night prior to driving to Baghdad, she was astonished that Amman was such a backwards city that it had no traffic lights.

"This is a highway," Raad explained, annoyed.

She complained that our five-star hotel wasn't quite to par. "You should see the hotels in Vegas. In Vegas, each hotel is the size of the city of Amman."

She insisted on using the hotel telephone to call her sister in America, even though her mother forbade her from doing so. Maysoon didn't listen, said it wasn't against the law to make a phone call. When she had the chance, she rushed to her room to do so. That's when Raad pulled me to the side and said that he'd blocked all the phone lines in our rooms because "this crazy one" – the name he started giving Maysoon – would otherwise jack up the hotel bill.

"But you're sane," he said. "So if you want to use the phone, that's fine. Let me know and we'll unblock it for you."

Raad continued to gripe about Maysoon as he limped from one spot to the other, occasionally stopping in front of the hotel mirrors to comb his hair. He had polio from when he was a child. Meanwhile, Maysoon continued to behave as if the Middle East was beneath her. From the moment Raad met Maysoon, he was certain that Maysoon was being forced into Iraq by her mother in an attempt to find her a husband because, he told me, "Who would marry her in America?"

Some Iraqi American girls who didn't have suitors knocking on their doors in the United States found a host of opportunities in Iraq. In my case, before I had even booked my ticket, I was approached by women who'd heard that I *may* be going to Iraq and wanted to introduce me to a son, brother, brother-in-law, nephew, or cousin, either to have a real marriage and settle down or, if I preferred, to have a fake marriage in order to bring the man into America, where each person would then go their separate ways. Why would I, or anyone else, break the law by faking a marriage? For humanitarian purposes, why else?

I was told that the men and women in Iraq have suffered tremendously through the Iraq/Iran War, then the 1991 Gulf War, then the long horrific sanctions. Surely, as an Iraqi-born woman and a follower of Christ, I could understand and sympathize with their suffering and would want to help rescue at least one Chaldean. And if I wanted to make some extra money doing this good deed, that was all right too. The man's family was willing to negotiate a price.

Well, I perfectly understood and fully sympathized with the Iraqis' suffering, but I had no plans of getting married in Iraq — not for real, not for fake, not for half-baked — so I quite easily got rid of these matchmakers, having become, at twenty-nine years old, an expert at that sort of thing.

Yes, Maysoon was a real character and was probably in search of a husband willing to marry just about anybody, but Raad himself wasn't that far behind her. In the airplane coming to Amman, just before takeoff, he'd spilt on the aisle floor an extra-large Coca-Cola cup which he'd picked up from the Little Caesar's in the airport's food court, only the cup did not contain Coca-Cola in it but rather jalapeno peppers. Once the peppers spread across the floor like an assembly toy with five thousand pieces, he immediately took off. The eyes and noses of passengers closest to the scene stung as the stewardesses looked up and down and all around to figure out where the jalapeno peppers had come from.

Maysoon had wasted time fretting that her menstrual pads would be discovered. Because Raad had bribed the custom officials, our luggage didn't go through the same horrendous searching that other unescorted passengers endured. Customs officials flipped through our US passports and nonchalantly chatted with Raad, who limped from one agent to the next, excited about the commotion at the border. Then we waited hours for our blood to be drawn to test if we had AIDS, in which case we wouldn't be able to enter Iraq.

"Doesn't it take days to get the results?" I asked.

"What do you think, this is real? It's a bunch of bullshit! They just want money."

Maysoon whimpered that making us wait for so long was not fair. She felt that as Arabs, we were being discriminated against. Had we been Americans, we would have been given special consideration.

Well, we are Americans, I wanted to tell her, but I figured

why bother? I looked behind me at the acres of sand and remembered my mother's words. "The Iraq in your head is not the Iraq in real life."

She had used every tactic she could to deter me from coming here. Who could blame her? This land was once partly occupied by the Ottoman Empire and the British Empire, and before that by tyrants like King Gilgamesh. Gilgamesh had later transformed into the best-known and most popular hero in the mythology of the ancient Near East, but tyranny continued to reside in Mesopotamia.

My mother did not want me to disrupt my American lifestyle by coming to Iraq, a war-torn country. In America, I led a safe and sound life as the family's video store manager who still lived, as tradition had it, under my mother's roof. The only time I was subjected to real danger, according to my most recent recollection, was one instance when my friend and I did our routine night walk in our upper middle-class neighborhood and heard a fierce roar from behind the bushes. We rushed home and witnessed a televised danger alert that a lion was roaming loose in our city.

The only sound advice I received from my mother was, "Don't expect to go to this trip on your own." But I already knew that. No foreigner in their right mind, especially not a woman, would make a trip to Iraq without a chaperone. Baghdad airport had been closed since the Persian Gulf War. For years the only route to get into Baghdad went like this: you flew into Amman, Jordan, and from there a car drove you into Baghdad through a fifteen- to seventeen-hour drive.

People visiting Iraq hired chaperones to get them from the US to Iraq. The most well-known chaperone in the community was Najib Shemami, a man who, as I write this in the summer of 2012, is sixty-two years old and is serving a four-year sentence in a federal prison in North Carolina. He was accused of being a spy for Iraq. Detroit newspapers described him as having "smuggled money, medicine and clothing into Iraq," although between 1996 and 2002, the time in which he traveled frequently to Iraq, the Chaldean American community knew him to "deliver" items to their relatives for a fee that was based on amount, weight, or quantity. These items included anything from videotapes of weddings and other ceremonies to Tylenol, makeup, clothes and shoes, toys, hair accessories, and peanut butter, a favorite with Christians during lent.

With the postal system no longer intact in Iraq, people didn't see the harm in giving their relatives gifts that put a smile on their faces and gave them hope and money to pay for their monthly expenses. Thanks to gifts sent to them from relatives in America, girls were able to put on rouge and wear new, though oftentimes hand-me-down, dresses; my cousin was able to get new brassieres, as brassieres had been banned from entering Iraq; men enjoyed some good-quality shoes; women were able to give their infants Tylenol or take a dose themselves if they had a headache from dealing with the children and from tolerating the stubborn sanctions; and someone who was fasting got to make a peanut butter sandwich. No serious crimes were committed, but back then, law said that it was a crime for US citizens, with the exception of persons in the White House, to deal with Iraq. Well, law didn't actually say the part about there being an exception to persons in the White House. I made that part up.

For about $400 per person, Najib also escorted groups of people into Iraq, delivering them and their luggage right to their relatives' footsteps. There were other men who played the role of smuggler and chaperone, but Najib had the reputation of being a real pro. In March of 2000, I tried to contact Najib, but I discovered that I'd just missed him. He'd left for Iraq a week or so prior and had had a full house. Spring was around the corner, which was a good time to visit Baghdad to avoid the unbearable summer heat that only Iraqis could bear and to celebrate Easter with relatives. It was a good time to see the motherland before the end of the world presented itself.

Someone recommended I contact Najib's younger brother, Raad Shemami. Raad had recently begun following in his brother's footsteps, but on a much smaller scale. Whereas Najib smuggled truckloads of items, Raad brought in a small suitcase. Whereas Najib brought along twenty to thirty people, Raad brought two or three. For Najib, this was a profitable business. For Raad, he often may have made only enough to cover his plane ticket. Najib was so big-time that he even had an advertisement in the Arab American and Chaldean Yellow pages that read:

> Najib Shemami, ready to transfer your wires
> and gifts to Jordan and also the motherland
> (Iraq) and to all governorates. Depend on
> him to put a smile on your relatives' faces. We
> have an office in Iraq ready to transfer your
> wires the same day and in trust.

This advertisement was translated from Arabic to

23

English, marked Government's Exhibit BW-86.5, and shown to a trial jury on September 12, 2008, at the US District Court in Detroit for a case that involved Dawn and Darrin Hanna.

CHAPTER 3
The Genius Brother

My friend's brother was the manager of KHRW (Kurdish Human Rights Watch), a refugee resettlement agency, and my friend asked me if I could help him set up the office. With Christians bearing the impact of animosity for what Muslims perceived as a "crusade" by the United States, as many as half a million Iraqi Christians escaped the sectarian fighting that resulted after the 2003 US-led invasion. In response, the US refugee program in 2007 began admitting Iraqis to the US, to date over 100,000 – the majority of which end up coming to Michigan. The State Department gave local resettlement agencies, like KHRW, an initial stipend of $900 to help each refugee with their immediate needs and to help finance the services provided by the aid groups.

The job at KHRW was easy, but there was no coffeemaker at the office, just a thermostat that brewed hot water. Every morning I stopped at a Dunkin' Donuts to grab a blueberry-flavored coffee, and one September morning, as I was paying for my coffee, Louie called and asked that I *please* call one of Hanna's family members, like Darrin, Dawn's brother.

This was not the first time Louie had called. Within days of our meeting at Sahara restaurant, he had contacted me an average of once a week, sometimes twice a week, reminding me of my promise to meet with the Hanna family. I had made one excuse after another, but that September morning, he said, "Weam, Dawn deserves to have her side of the story heard."

"And what good would that do?"

"Who knows? It might get her some media attention and later affect the appellate judges' decision."

I was quiet. In the Chaldean community, when someone asks for help, especially with a serious matter, another Chaldean must respond, or at least try to. My conscience, the cumulative effect of his phone calls, and the fact that this story kept pursuing me like a stray cat in need of food, caused me to cave in. I wrote down Darrin's number on the back of the Dunkin' Donuts receipt. In the car, I called Darrin, and we agreed to have coffee the following week. He said he would meet me at Big Boy Restaurant once he got out of class from Oakland University, and I asked him to email me the link to Dawn's website.

Justice4DawnHanna.com, which no longer exists, had a picture of Dawn. She was a little heavyset with the typical dark and exotic features of a Middle Easterner. One hand on the hip and the other hip tilted to the side, she had the attitude and grin of her Uncle Raad. There was a summary of Dawn's case; links to a local television and newspaper coverage of the story; letters sent to the Judge who sentenced Dawn and to the prosecutor who prosecuted her; letters to Michigan Senators' offices; and a letter to President Obama who, according to the director of the Office of Presidential Correspondence, receives 65,000 paper letters every week and about 100,000 emails, 1,000 faxes, and some 2,500 to 3,500 phone calls per day.

I googled the name Dawn Hanna and found an article published by the Oakland Press with the headline, "Traitor or Victim? Family works to appeal conviction of woman they say is innocent of treason." I quickly skimmed through the article, scrolled down, and read the comments posted by readers.

> Comment: Go back home terrorists! "I did not know I was doing business with Iraq" is not a valid excuse. Maybe her business deals with Iraq put US military soldiers at an increased risk.
>
> Response: Guess who sold Saddam chemicals, WMDs and other military goods while he fought the Iranians? Will give you a hint; begins with U and ends with A. U.A.
>
> Comment: Iraqis are scums.
>
> Response: She is not Iraqi scum. She's American born and Catholic. Check your facts.

As I stared at the screen, I wondered when Iraq-related painful stories would stop following me like ghosts. After my visit in 2000, I never returned to Iraq. Another big war had broken out in 2003, and Iraq, once almost free of crime, especially horrific random killings, was now considered the number one most dangerous country in the world. Its rich history and its oil reserves were buried even further beneath the ground as violence, misery, confusion, and corruption occupied the land from every angle. The 2003 US occupation led to a civil war that claimed the lives of some 500,000 civilians.

During the invasion, the Iraqi borders were left wide open, so no one had to knock on the doors to be allowed inside. Al-Qaeda, Kurdish rebels, Turkish troops, Sunni and Shiite insurgents from Saudi Arabia, Morocco, Egypt, Syria, Yemen, and all over the Arab world just packed up their explosive devices, artilleries, and mines and walked right into Iraq, set up camp and militias, and began formulating plots to kidnap, rape, and slaughter people, children included, and to bomb and destroy places with mind-numbing regularity, causing 2.5 million Iraqis to flee to neighboring countries and another 2.2 million in Iraq to be internally displaced.

The insurgency started a massacre and forced an immigration and refugee crisis on the Christians like no other in Iraq's history. They turned what once was the Garden of Eden to a hell on earth.

* * *

Big Boy Restaurant was crowded Tuesday evening. Darrin called and said he was running late. I sat in one of the booths and ordered a coffee. I looked around as I waited. Although

I was not hungry, the steam that rose from the dinner buffet tempted me to dip my finger into the chafer, if only to grab a biscuit. The smell of chicken broccoli soup near the salad bar made me want to go home and cuddle up with a cup of soup. And the garden room to the right side of the restaurant would be a nice place to take off my sandals, put my feet up on the booth, and lay against the wall, where the sun embraced that whole section.

"Hi, Weam." I heard the voice of a man behind me.

As I turned around, I realized Darrin had already taken a seat across from me. In his early thirties, Darrin was tall and nicely built, with his father's and uncles' wide faces, but not quite as wide. His dark features resembled that of his sister's, but unlike his sister, he looked more like a European than a Middle Easterner.

"Sorry I'm late," he said, frazzled. "My class ran ten minutes over and the traffic on M- 59 was really bad."

He was forty-five minutes late.

The waitress came to our table. He ordered a coffee, then pointed at my cup. "Did you want anything else?"

"I'm all set." I took my pen and opened my spiral notebook. "Do you mind if we start? Because..."

"Oh, yes, yes, please." He patted down his hair and straightened his shirt collar.

I recounted what I understood so far about the case. A businessman in the UK named Emad called Dawn one day and asked her to broker telecommunications equipment for Turkey. As a broker, Dawn was like a middleman, a real estate agent, bringing a buyer and seller together. What Emad asked Dawn to do was legal, but then it turned out that the equipment was intended for Iraq, and that made it illegal because of the embargo on Iraq. Dawn had always maintained she believed the equipment was going to Turkey and nowhere else.

"That's what her clients had us believe," Darrin said.

"There was someone other than Emad?"

"His partner, Walid."

"Who's Walid?"

"He worked for Dresser International, which once was a subsidiary of Halliburton."

"Dick Cheney's Halliburton!?"

"Yes."

"Oh."

"There were a lot of government people involved in this deal, but since it's under seal, we don't know exactly who they are. The government spent four and a half years investigating this case and finding ways to twist the truth so they can hide facts from the defense," he said, emphasizing his words the way a teacher would when lecturing to her students. "They never told us or our attorneys or the jury that my sisters' clients were CIA operatives participating in a secret US operation intended to listen in on, through this telecom equipment, Saddam and his regime."

When Darrin spoke, all the traits Americans were known to have – openness and simplicity – poured forth like a sweet fragrance that left its imprint on well-dressed passersby. But I felt like there was something he wasn't telling me.

"Darrin, there must have been evidence that made the jury convict her."

"The government took thousands and thousands of my

sister's emails from over tons of business transactions that spanned over five years, shuffled them around, and created a story that made my sister look guilty."

"What did these emails say?"

"In one of them she talks about sending other items to Iraq, like cigarettes, because she thought she could. If they wanted to charge her for something, they should have charged her for an export violation, not a conspiracy charge! I mean, who did she conspire with? Emad, the guy working for the US government? Me? Well, the jury said I'm innocent. So who did she conspire with? If you are going to be charged of conspiracy, shouldn't there be a co-conspirator?"

I put the question mark at the end of the sentence and looked over my notes. "I want to ask about your uncle, but can you first tell me what exactly is telecommunication equipment?"

"It's a network that allows people to use mobile phones. You can do nothing with it as they had bought it. You would need to install software or hook it up to an existing network, which Iraq didn't have. Keep in mind, this equipment was not prohibited from entering Iraq. It was permitted under the Oil-for-Food program, but first you had to get a license by filling out a two-page application."

He waited for me to finish taking notes. The waitress returned and refilled our coffees.

"My sister was fined $1.1 million and sentenced six years. She is only the second person in US history to be sentenced to prison time for violating the US embargo on Iraq. The funny thing is people were constantly smuggling things in who never got tried, like Dick Cheney."

US firms routinely used foreign subsidiaries and joint ventures to skirt the sanctions, not just with Iraq but with other countries like Indonesia, Libya, Iran, Nigeria, and Azerbaijan. One of those firms was Halliburton. Once he became head of Halliburton in 1995, Cheney promised to maintain a hard line against Baghdad. Yet UN records show that two subsidiaries of Halliburton sold water and sewage treatment pumps, spare parts for oil facilities, and pipeline equipment to Baghdad through French affiliates from 1997 to 2000. Two former senior executives of the Halliburton subsidiaries said that, as far as they knew, there was no policy against doing business with Iraq. One of the executives also said that he was certain Cheney knew about their Iraqi contracts.

"I don't really get what the government would gain by giving her such a harsh sentence," I said.

"They labeled her case a national security threat which heightened the seriousness of the crime. My sister, an all-American girl from Rochester Hills, Michigan," he said, gesturing up and down with wide open arms, as if lifting weights, "was putting the United States under threat when this whole operation was to help the United States! And from what we and some people from the government learned later, we believe that this operation was financed by Dick Cheney. Of course, we can't get to the bottom of it because it's, again, all sealed."

Sealed records are not public records. Once a record is sealed, in some states, the contents are legally considered never to have occurred and can even be destroyed. Records commonly sealed are birth records for closed adoption, juvenile criminal records, witness protection information, and cases involving trade and state records. On rare occasions, although it became a more common practice after the 9/11 attacks, the government requests a case to be filed under seal because of classified information that could result in damage to national security if it were disclosed to the wrong person. For instance, twenty-eight pages of the 9/11 Commission remain sealed despite efforts from the families of 9/11 victims, lawmakers, and others to declassify them. It is believed that these pages show that Saudi Arabia supported the hijackers.

"What about your uncle, Najib Shemami? I did some research and found that he pled guilty to being a spy for Saddam."

"My uncle saying he's a spy is like him saying he's a rocket scientist. If anything, he was infiltrating the coffee shop on Seven Mile just to be on good terms with the customs agents in Iraq."

In 1999, the Chaldean Federation of America declared the Seven Mile area in Detroit as "Chaldean Town," although today hardly any Chaldeans live there.

"My uncle can't even read a food menu. When we were younger we would go to a restaurant and he'd always tell the waitress, 'What are your specials today?' She'd go down a list of main courses and he'd just pick from that. He'd say, 'Yeah, the fish sounds good!' I used to wonder, why doesn't he look over the menu instead? I asked my dad one day and he said it's because he can't read English."

As I tried to catch up on the note-taking, I couldn't help but overhear the loud man behind us say to the waitress, "He was caught eating pistachios in the store without paying for them, and the guy is a billionaire!" The woman sitting with him added, "And his wife puts her makeup in Ziploc bags."

"My uncle had tried to get Dawn involved in his deals, but knowing how he did business, she never agreed to it," Darrin continued, and I pulled myself away from wondering why a billionaire would eat pistachios without paying for them. "I think this angered him. You see, my dad's side of the family are...well, let's just say that my dad is the best one out of them and that his older brother Najib is the black sheep. But hey, for winning a case against my sister and my uncle, even though there was clearly a Brady violation with my sister, the main prosecutor in their cases received a promotion to US General Attorney shortly after Dawn's trial."

"What's a Brady Violation?"

"It's when the government fails to disclose evidence to the defense, therefore depriving the defendant of a fair trial."

"So where's the case at now?"

"After we learned of the new information, Dawn's attorney filed a motion for a new trial. It was denied. The Judge found the CIA's involvement – which was Dawn's conspiracy charge – not important enough to warrant a new trial. I guess the prosecutor is worried that releasing my sister would kill her trying-to-protect-the-country image."

I thought about President Bush and his noble mission to "disarm Iraq, to free its people, and to defend the world from grave danger," which took the lives of thousands of military men and women and brought Iraq to ruins.

"I thought, wow, if this could happen to us, this could happen to anyone," he said. "If our founding fathers heard about this case, they'd turn in their graves. Like my own father, our forefathers left their countries and came to the

United States because of oppression and this type of abuse of power. The United States is supposed to be a country that runs on checks and balances. Yet prosecutors have complete autonomy, are free to do what they want. There's not a deterrent."

I noticed some people in the nearby tables turn their heads toward us. Darrin's voice was loud, though not in an obnoxious way. He wasn't yelling. He simply spoke with the ease of someone having a heated discussion in the privacy of their own home. I wondered if he naturally spoke like that, or if he'd intended for the world to hear what he had to say.

"In fact, it is in their best interest that they prosecute as many people as possible so they can have a thick resume. So rather than catching the kingpin of a drug operation, for instance, they go after the lowest hanging fruit, many of whom are mentally ill or poverty stricken, the people who don't make a dent in the drug business because the kingpins will just replace them with another drug runner. Then the prosecutor will mention as their accomplishment the conviction of 423 drug dealers. Of course, they're not going to go after the kingpin because it takes real work, and you might go for five years and never get them. That doesn't look good on your resume."

I didn't know how to feel about this case. I was accustomed to governments cooking up an excuse to enter into a war, but cooking up a case to put someone in prison was all new to me.

"The government not only endangered my sister's life by pulling her into a CIA operation, but they prosecuted her as if she was helping the enemy. They put her in prison even though two of the CIA operatives risked their lives and the lives of their families by coming forward to tell the truth. The operatives were outraged that the government swept their testimonies under the rug."

The system was evidently a well-established bee colony, and trying to play the role of the beekeeper without the proper suit or equipment could be quite dangerous. As an Iraqi American woman with a young family to care for, it would be unwise to get involved. My husband and I had already experienced our share of racial profiling and discrimination from immigration enforcement, and it was far from over. The last thing we needed was added scrutiny.

"What does your family think I can do for Dawn?" I asked.

"The case is under appeal. We hoped that you can bring attention to this case through a book, which would put pressure on the government to revert the court's decision or release my sister on bond until the government completes its investigation. A number of government officials we recently met with in Washington have suggested we do that."

I was quiet. The last thing I wanted to do was get involved in a political story, but something about the way in which Darrin kept calling Dawn "my sister" melted my heart away. I was the eleventh of twelve children – four boys and seven girls – so from the weight he placed on those words, "my sister," I knew how much love there was between him and Dawn and how much pain sat in his heart.

"A book can take years," I said. "You guys are looking for a fast route."

"Yes, we are. My sister is afraid that if she completes her

six-year sentence, she will be forty-two years old by the time she gets out and maybe unable to start a family."

"I'll need Dawn's mailing address and the court transcripts," I said, gathering my writing material and my purse. It was time to return home. "I must do more research to figure out how, or if, I can help."

"Whatever you can do, we would really appreciate it. This thing has wiped us all out."

We walked outside. It was still daylight, and there was a light breeze causing the nearby tree branches to rustle. We stood in front of my minivan, next to the chubby boy statue wearing red-and-white checkered overalls and holding a double-decker cheeseburger.

As we said goodbye, Darrin once again apologized for being forty-five minutes late. "A few of my students approached me after class and it was hard to just walk away."

Surprised, I took another look at him. "You teach at Oakland University?"

"I'm an engineering professor."

"I thought you were a student."

He laughed. "Yeah, I get that a lot. I got my PhD at an earlier age than most people."

I remembered Louie telling me that people called Darrin a genius.

"Is it true that you worked to find safe spots for people to go to before a hurricane hits?"

"Yes, and I also worked to find advanced treatment services for the mentally ill. But when I was indicted, I took a leave of absence from teaching and I had to stop all the beneficial work I was involved in."

"Have you gone back to this work?"

"The projects were funded by grants. Even though I was acquitted, I got a letter from the Defense Logistics Agency telling me that I was debarred for ten years from government contracting. I fought this, and the debarment was reduced to three years."

I stood dumbfounded and stared at him as if he were a bizarre creature. He smiled, placing his hands in his pockets. "I'm sure the American people would've liked future Katrina issues solved more than having me indicted or putting Dawn in prison," he said, as if reading my thoughts.

I later learned that Darrin received many awards and honors for his work, even a teacher of the year award. He developed software called Next Step solution that aids doctors in coordinating the treatment of the mentally ill. He created a financial literacy program for children, which taught them how to save and develop savings accounts. He was able to pass a resolution through the state house making financial literacy for students grades K-12 mandatory. I decided Louie was not exaggerating when he'd called Darrin a genius.

CHAPTER 4
The American Flag is Left in Rest

There is a Barnes & Noble in Rochester Hills just north of the busy intersection of Auburn and Rochester Road, which has been there for over twenty years. Between 2000 and 2002, when Dawn was working on the telecommunication deal, and around 2004 to 2007, when she and her brother were being investigated, indicted, and put on trial, Dawn had studied and hung out at that Barnes & Noble. Some nights, the employees had to throw her out, not literally, because the store would be closing.

On a Wednesday, Thursday, Friday, or Saturday night, you would find her there, in the New Age Section, or Religious Studies, Gourmet Food, Music, or Magazine/Business sections, sitting in the middle of the aisle, a cup of coffee or a bottle of water beside her. She was totally engrossed in the worlds of yoga, meditation, the positive power of the universe, natural healing, essential oils, Pilates, and body wraps.

Nothing could snatch her attention away from those lovely therapeutic methods of healing, many of which were part of her ancient Mesopotamian heritage, where thousands of years ago hundreds of different healing drugs were used by physicians, priests, and sorcerers.

"Dawn is like a magician with a crystal ball," her friend Louie said to me during one of our phone conversations when he had tried to convince me to call Dawn's family. "She's a powerful spirit and can do whatever she sets her mind to."

I wasn't surprised or scared by that. In parts of Mesopotamian religion, magic was believed in and actively practiced in order to influence one's success, health, and wealth. At the city of Uruk, archaeologists have excavated houses dating from the fifth and fourth centuries BCE in which cuneiform clay tablets have been unearthed containing magical chants.

Dawn and I might have crossed paths at this bookstore. Barnes & Noble used to be my sanctuary for over two decades, where, with a latte in hand, I came to read and write or attend the writer's group meetings held every third Thursday of the month.

One day, outside of the bookstore, way in the back, I had discovered a fence covered with grape leaves. Each leaf was big enough to stuff a pork chop in, and they were not bitten by worms or torn apart by bad weather, had no galls or mildew. I hurriedly informed my mother and sisters of what I'd found and that same day, we all squeezed into my minivan, empty plastic grocery bags in our hands, and drove to the back of the store. My daughter sat in a stroller and watched – she must have been a year or so – as we excitedly picked the grape leaves, studying them like archaeologists who'd discovered a hidden treasure, commenting on their cleanliness and tenderness, their perfect size, their secret location that had not been discovered by other Chaldean housewives, as those women were not the type to go to a bookstore.

We were plucking away when a tall, well-dressed man suddenly appeared from around the corner. He was the manager of the bookstore, and he hesitantly approached us and asked what we were doing. He looked a little nervous. We had all been dressed in black because my aunt, the one whose house I'd stayed at during my trip to Iraq, had recently passed away and we were in mourning for forty days. Obviously the sight of us frightened the store manager, so we explained that during summer we picked grape leaves, enough to last throughout the winter, to make an Iraqi dish called dolma. Dolma consists of stuffed grape leaves as well as other stuffed vegetables such as cabbage, onions, green peppers, eggplants, tomatoes, potatoes, or whatever one wanted to stuff.

He was nice about it, said that was fine, but he asked that we inform someone in the store next time we decide to pick grape leaves so they won't be surprised by our sudden presence.

On a rainy evening in September, I met Dawn's mother, Linda, at the Barnes & Noble in Rochester. Darrin suggested I pick up the transcripts from her, as her schedule was more flexible. He took a lot of trips related to his work, which included trying to get his sister out of prison.

When I entered the bookstore, Linda stood at the coffee shop's checkout counter. She was a tall, heavyset woman with strawberry blonde hair and ivory colored skin. We had never met before, but we were able to spot each other. Aside from the place being almost empty, I definitely passed for a woman of Middle Eastern heritage because of my dark complexion. She was of German and Irish heritage and looked like one of those hardcore moms who cook and bake and make everyone around them feel nice and cozy. We introduced ourselves and made our orders. We grabbed our cups and, on our way to an empty table, I noticed she was limping.

"This is my dinner," she said, sitting down and pointing to her large cold drink. "I don't like to cook anymore because there is no one to cook for."

Something about Linda immediately made me feel sorry for her. I'm sure the fact that within the past two years, two of her children had been indicted and, for a year, her daughter had been locked up had a lot to do with how I felt. But there was something else – the absence of an ego. When she said "I," there was no boasting, selfishness, manipulation or the need to control you, but just a telling of a story. Her soul was gone but yet still here, like the Greek statues that continue to stand on the grounds of Athens despite the god or goddesses they personify having long been buried.

We did not talk about the case right away. I first asked her how she had met Toby, Dawn's father. She told me they were at a soccer game. He was a member of the team, and that day he came in late so the coach told him to sit on the bleachers. Toby sat next to Linda, they began to talk, and soon they were married and had three children: Dean, Dawn, and Darrin. Fourteen years later they got a divorce, but even though both remarried, they always maintained a good relationship for the sake of their children. Toby and Rick, Linda's second husband, even got along great. They went up north alone to hunt, and after Rick died of cancer...

She did not finish her story. She suddenly broke into tears. "That's why I swore at Rick for leaving me in such a mess." She wiped her eyes and nose with a napkin. "I'm sorry. I don't know why I'm telling you all this. It's just that...this whole thing has ruined our family."

I felt terrible and awkward about asking her what I wanted to ask. Once I saw that she was composed, I said, "Linda, the government does not pick people at random. Why did they go after Dawn to begin with?"

"There's a bigger picture to all of this," she said, tightening her eyes. "Toby's older brother, Najib, the one who is accused of spying for Saddam. He called and threatened me... well, let's go back to 2003, 2004. He wanted to do business with Dawn and Darrin, but they said no because they didn't like the way he did business. So he said, 'I'm going to destroy Dawn and Darrin and their company.' Years passed, and one day, I got a phone call on my way to court when they were choosing the jurors for the grand jury. Najib said, 'Linda, we've got to meet. This has gone too far.' But Toby warned me not to meet with him, so I didn't. Later, the chairman of the Chaldean Federation said to me, 'I know that Najib testified and lied about Dawn to the prosecution so he would get off. But that's all sealed.'"

Najib Shemami pled guilty to providing military information to the Iraqi Intelligence Service under the government of Saddam Hussein and was sentenced to forty-six months imprisonment. According to documents filed in court, Najib traveled to Iraq, met with officers of the Iraqi Intelligence

Service, and allegedly reported information relating to the "activities of Iraqi expatriates in the United States who were opposed to Saddam Hussein," many of whom were otherwise known in Iraq as communists. The relatively strong communist parties in Iraq are never mentioned in the United States. They are simply grouped with other anti-Saddamists.

Najib also reported information about potential candidates for political office in Iraq, otherwise known as Iranians. By 2010, with the presence of Iraqi Prime Minister Nouri Al-Malika, Iran was in charge of Iraq. Since the 1960s, Al-Maliki has been a member of the Dawa Party, which backed the Iranian Revolution and also Ayatollah Khomeini during the Iran-Iraq war. The Dawa Party was widely viewed in the West as a terrorist organization. In 1982, Dawa members attempted to assassinate then President Saddam Hussein in the city of Dujail. They failed. In response, Saddam ordered the killing of 148 men.

The assassination attempt happened during the first two years of the Iran-Iraq war, and it was carried out by what we term here in the United States, under similar circumstances, "terrorists" groups. Twenty-four years later, Saddam was tried and hanged for this act because, according to the 2013 website of Council on Foreign Relations, Dawa is no longer on the US Department's list of terrorist organizations. After the end of the 1980-88 Iran-Iraq war, more moderate branches of Dawa began to gain ascendance. The website claims that "Dawa is widely *believed* to have ended its terrorist activities by about 1990." However, since statistics show that only 8 percent of people keep their New Year's resolutions, this might not be a very realistic claim.

"Najib was sentenced over a year ago," she said, "but he still has not served one day of his forty-six month prison term. He received extensions three times, once to attend his son's wedding, a second time for some bullshit excuse, and a third time for another bullshit excuse, claiming he has cancer."

"When the government began the investigation, did you think they were after Najib?"

"No! We thought they were after Emad, the CIA operative. It was his deal! And that one company, Dresser, which is somehow tied to Dick Cheney. With this project, we found that anyone associated with the government stayed sound and safe, but with us, ten men in bullet proof vests barged into our office and arrested Dawn and Darrin. My children's pictures were plastered on all the news channels, next to Saddam's pictures, with the heading 'Brother and Sister Indicted for Doing Business with Saddam.' My children have never even been to Iraq! They don't even speak Arabic. Dawn knows a few words here and there, but that's about it."

She told me how active Darrin was about trying to get Dawn out of prison. He had meetings lined up with government officials, whether in Detroit or Washington DC. The year prior, he teamed up with Ron Scott, an activist who worked closely with Congressman John Conyers's office, and they took a trip to Washington together. They planned on going again.

She described Dawn and Darrin's relationship. Even though Darrin was five years younger than Dawn, they were once best friends. They worked together, travelled together, went to parties, restaurants, the movies together. There were pictures of them at social events on their computer screen at work.

"It's not like that anymore," she said, shaking her head in regret. "Now they fight over me, each one accusing the other of being the reason why I got sick last May, and threatening that if something were to happen to me, the other is to blame."

In May 2010, Linda had a mini-stroke due to stress and was in the hospital for five days. She lost comprehension of what had happened for the last nine months. The doctor said this could happen again, and they put her on medication. Darrin was scared he would lose his mother. To protect her, he blocked her phone from receiving Dawn's calls so she could be more detached from stressful situations, but Linda found a way to go around that and unblocked it.

"I can't – I can't not pick up! She's my daughter!" Cupping her face with her hands, Linda sobbed like a little girl, like my little girl. I reached out and caressed her wrist. "If I could get political asylum for Dawn somewhere, I would. But it usually works the other way around. People come to the United States for political asylum. So we have to take this rollercoaster ride with government officials who make one promise after another, but they don't deliver."

She mentioned the names of several people who'd promised they'd release Dawn, including a man named Fred. Fred lived in Washington, DC and had worked with counterintelligence for over thirty years. He had met Toby in Baghdad when Toby was serving as an advisor and translator for the US Army. And then there was the woman from Congressman John Conyers's office, Elisa.

"Elisa said that yes, the congressman was aware of this case and yes, he's taking it on and yes, she'd have Dawn home for her birthday on November 30. Then she promised, 'Oh, it'll be by Christmas.' She said she will go to the prison herself and pick Dawn up. That's how we spent Christmas last year. Darrin lived with his phone. He waited and waited and waited for that phone to ring, but the call never came. We thought maybe Dawn will walk through that door and surprise us because Elisa promised. After Christmas, that woman dropped off the face of the earth. I'd contact her and she wouldn't respond."

Linda nervously twirled her fingers around the straw in the cup. "One thing I've learned from all this is that the government, especially the CIA and FBI, does not have to answer for anything. They have complete immunity."

Prior to the Dawn Hanna case, all I really knew about the FBI and the CIA was that if you were of Iraqi descent, were fluent in Arabic, met certain requirements, and passed the security enhancement test, you could get a good paying job with full benefits, but you'd likely need to relocate, especially when working with the CIA, as confidentiality was a top issue for them. I learned all this on March 11, 2009, when I was six months pregnant with my second child.

Accompanied by my sister and my three-year-old daughter, I attended a career fair at Shenandoah Country Club that was held by the army, FBI, and CIA. I had just returned from a three-day tour of Fort Jackson army base in South Carolina, where I and about 200 other leaders, journalists, and media professionals from the Middle Eastern and Arab communities were brought together as COFs (Center of Influence) people to "increase army awareness and improve COI relationships in support of the United States Army Recruiting Command (USAREC) recruiting mission."

I was very impressed with the tour in Fort Jackson, the politeness and mannerisms of everyone around me, their hospitality, good humor and dignified attitude toward their work. Feeling the heaviness of my pregnant body, I also envied the young men and women who climbed walls and nets and ran around the military base.

I had always appreciated the disciplinary ways of the military, no less now that I was a wife and a mother. Since my college days, I had often considered joining. I loved the intense training, the uniforms, the benefits, the transformation I saw in those who had gone into the military and the remarkable difference between them and those who did not go. The problem was that I wasn't crazy about the idea of killing. When I watched a bull fight in Mexico and saw the bull die at the hands of the Matador, I was in tears. And like it or not, killing was part of the package when joining the military. So at the Career Fair, I wondered if I could find something useful to do without having to hold a gun and shoot anyone.

"Mom, look! It's Obama!" my daughter, one month short of turning three, shouted when an African American man from the FBI went up to the podium. The people behind us laughed. Due to the excitement I displayed when I learned about Obama's 2009 win, my daughter began to shout "Look, Mom, it's Obama!" whenever any African American man came on the television screen or passed us by in the supermarket or other public places.

So that was all I knew about the FBI and the CIA. Oh,

and I also knew that the CIA and Saddam were once very close friends, starting in the late 1950s or so, when the CIA began rearing him and the Baath Party into power.

The sound of rain started drumming against the bookstore's rooftop. Through the glass door I saw a dark shadow appear over the trees and parking lot. There were trickles of grayish lightening. The sun suddenly went away, and the inside of the store grew dim. I felt cold. I needed to leave and pick up my husband and children from my in-law's house nearby, but I felt sorry for this woman and wished I could pick her up like china and mend the broken pieces.

Tears rolled down Linda's face as she described the way in which Dawn, a free spirit since she was born, was now in a cage, in a cubbyhole, digging for a hole to get out. "The reason Dawn cannot get herself to fit in at a prison is because she is not guilty. She was railroaded and used as a scapegoat."

While every word she said saddened me – like how she refused to go out with family and friends, didn't want anything other than to have her daughter home, how she always told her son that everything was all right when really most of the time she barely had any money – what struck me the most was the story about the American flag that used to always fly outside her home. These days the pole was empty.

"Rick was always in search of the ultimate flag pole," she said, tears once again forming in her eyes, "so it would be a nice sturdy one. The kids gave him his first one on Christmas, along with the flag. And every time the flag got tattered, we would do just as we were raised to do; we folded and burned it and never let it touch the ground." She started biting her nail and broke down. "Unfortunately, I can't bring myself to fly an American flag…when I think that this country has turned their back on my daughter and others that are in the same situation. So I cannot fly an American flag. It's just left in rest."

CHAPTER 5
The Forgotten Sanctions

Cran-Hill Ranch is a Christian family campground and retreat ministry located in northern Michigan. Near the campground is Hillview Lake and Cranberry Lake, where one can swim, rent a boat, or fish from the small dock. The campground has a petting farm, horse and pony rides, wagon rides, rock climbing, shooting range, archery and Sunday Mass. I found this place online, and because there was a cancellation on Labor Day weekend, my family, immediate and otherwise, was able to reserve the Stone House.

Linda gave me the court transcripts on a CD file. Some three thousand pages, all PDF. The first chance I got, I took the CD to Kinko's to get it all printed but was told that the material wouldn't be ready until the next day. I barely made it there the first time, on a stormy day, with the kids strapped in the car. I doubted I'd have enough time to return again. I ended up taking my laptop to the weekend family trip at

Cran-Hill Ranch despite the large number of children tagging along and the chance of something spilling or falling on
my laptop.

According to MapQuest, the drive would take three
hours, eleven minutes. We got lost along the way for over an
hour. Many griped about the extra time spent on the road,
but I did not mind it. I happily sat in the back of the minivan,
the computer on my lap, and read the court transcripts.

"What are you doing, Weam?" my mother asked. She
was sitting in the passenger seat, beside my husband. He was
driving.

"She's doing her homework," my husband said, smiling
and looking at me through the rearview mirror. "She has a
test tomorrow."

I ignored him and kept reading.

When we arrived at the Cran-Hill Ranch campground,
we did not know where to go. It was 300 acres of rolling hills
and 50 buildings. A truck slowed down for us.

"Good afternoon!" one of the men said.

"Where's the main office?" my husband asked. "We need
to pick up the key for the house we're renting."

"Are you the Yatooma's?"

"Yes."

"Hello, I'm Joe," the driver said. "You can stay here and
we'll bring you the key."

We parked the car. Most got out of the cars to stretch
their legs and look around. Some of the children cried about
there not being a pool or water resort in sight. I could see and
smell the petting farm across from the dirt road in front of
us. I was excited to take my son there.

"Look at this beautiful house," my sister said, looking behind us. I and a few others followed the direction of her eyes. A quaint, big stone house with large windows stood there. Eight wide steps led to the front burgundy door. A charcoal grill was at the bottom of the steps.

"Let me show you around," said the man who returned with our key after he shook hands with my husband and my brothers.

It turned out the stone house we so admired was where we were going to stay. It could hold eighteen people and had a heated porch with four tables that sat a total of twenty people. The men of the family brought the heavy stuff down from the car and into the house. The women made sure to keep a close watch on the children as they chose the sleeping arrangements for the four bedrooms upstairs. They then brought the food to the kitchen. One of my sisters-in-law insisted she first wipe the counters and cupboards.

We went on the wagon ride, visited the petting zoo, and took a long walk on the wooden trail. We guessed whether some plants were grape leaves or not. They were not, so we kept walking. That evening, those in charge of the camp set up picnic tables in front of the campground store and passed out free ice cream.

The men later went to a nearby Meijer to buy meat and poultry for our late dinner barbecue. While the women prepared the salads and appetizers, the children went on top of the four tables in the green patio room and belly danced to loud Arabic songs.

The whole time I carried my laptop around as though it was a book. Reading further into the transcripts, I remem-

bered what Darrin had said about the trial being complicated, that no way the average Joe, otherwise known as the
juror, could comprehend all its ins and outs. Well, that was
no surprise. The Dawn Hanna case was about breaking an
embargo, and if few Americans knew that Iraq, the cradle of
civilization and the birthplace of Prophet Abraham, existed,
hardly anyone had heard about the embargo that went on for
almost thirteen years, even though it cost the lives of at least
500,000 children, almost three times as many as the number of Japanese killed during the US atomic bomb attacks.
So I found it odd that, before the start of the Hanna trial, the
Judge encouraged the jurors not to take notes.

"There is paper available for you in the jury room," the
Judge said, "but you will find that your collective memory in
the end will serve you well in remembering facts."

Dawn's case was overloaded with mundane, although
crucial, information. It was not exciting to read, and surely
not that fun to watch. I was later told that two jurors had fall-
en asleep. No wonder. Who could blame them? The trial was
boring, and that boringness dragged on for over three weeks.
No one died or was punched in the face or even pinched in
this so-called crime. No money or property was stolen, no
one was sexually molested, and no attempt to betray a country, overthrow a government, or assassinate a president was
in sight.

Specialists were flown into the courtroom from different parts of the country or from overseas to talk about and
describe in elaborate details the telecommunication equipment, the financial transactions, the waybill used for the
shipment, and the Oil-for-Food program. This information

didn't cause any hullaballoo, but it made me want to bang my head against the wall. Had I not known the part about the CIA operatives, which the government had kept hidden from the jury, I might have done just that.

The parts that did not bore me were the ones where the sanctions were used to destroy yet one more person of Iraqi heritage, as if they hadn't done enough damage already. The UN sanctions against Iraq began months before the Gulf War, on August 6, 1990, the forty-fifth anniversary of the Hiroshima atomic bombing, when President George H.W. Bush issued Executive Order 12722, finding "that the policies and actions of the Government of Iraq constitute an unusual and extraordinary threat to the national security and foreign policy of the United States."

The Iraqi sanctions were the strictest and most devastating in the history of the UN. If an American citizen in the 1990s tried to send food and medicine to the Iraqi people as free gifts, something the UN sanctions allowed, that generous action was prohibited by US law. The US statutes used to enforce the UN sanctions were older and more rigid than the Security Council's Resolution 661 but were not updated to allow for the resolution's humanitarian exemption. The sanctions were considered by many, including former UN humanitarian aid coordinator in Iraq, Denis Halliday, to be one of the decade's greatest crimes, as horrendous as Bosnia or Rwanda. Halliday resigned in 1998 after launching a scathing attack on the sanctions policy, calling it genocide. A few years later, his successor, Hans von Sponeck, also resigned, outraging London and Washington by saying that the sanctions had created a "true human tragedy."

Initially the sanctions were imposed to punish Iraq for invading Kuwait. They were kept in place after the Gulf War, supposedly in order to pressure Saddam to disarm. Later their goal was to remove Saddam from power, which was as insurmountable a task as asking the US and British governments to relax the sanctions, if only to facilitate the purchase of food, medicines, and other essential supplies. What the sanctions intended to do was one thing and what they actually did was another. Approximately a million Iraqis, half of which were children under the age of five, died from malnutrition or inadequate health care resulting from economic sanctions.

The sanctions also kept Iraq from operating in the world economy, which was crippling to a country recovering from war. Its economy spiraled downward, and the value of its currency crashed. The Iraqi dinar was worth $3.22 US Dollars in 1991. After the first Gulf War, the dinar dropped in value to approximately $0.22 under the US Embargo and kept plummeting down to where 2900 dinars were worth one dollar. Before the sanctions, the average Iraqi employee, say a teacher, for example, made seven hundred dinars a month, equivalent to $2254, and had little expenses because gas and food were very cheap, and so were the electricity, water, and telephone bills. In Iraq, people didn't have mortgage payments because homes were bought in full, cash up-front. So unless you rented a house from someone, which was also usually cheap, you simply paid a small property tax at the end of the year. After the Gulf War, the average salary for everyone, including doctors, was three to four dollars a month.

At Cran-Hill Ranch, we attended a liturgy in the out-
door woods. We walked up a long hill to get to the Lodge,
where a free breakfast of pancakes was served. Whenever
possible, I returned to reading the transcripts, and each time
Iraq, the Gulf War, the sanctions, and the 2003 US-led invasion were mentioned by anyone in the courtroom during the
trial, I revisited the trip I'd taken to Iraq in 2000, chaperoned
by Dawn's uncle, Raad.

CHAPTER 6
What Real Crimes Look Like

"This is Baghdad," Raad said after long hours of riding in silence.

Maysoon simply glanced toward the window with her droopy eyes. She was worn out by the seventeen-hour drive. Her mother stretched her arms and twisted her back side to side. I stared outside, my fingertips at the edge of the van's window. "The city doesn't look like it has gone through a war," I said. "It's all intact."

"Saddam fixed a lot of it up – on the outside," Raad said.

"Because of the sanctions, the Iraqi government is limited to how much oil it can sell and how many spare parts it can import," said the driver. He had not spoken to us – only to Raad – throughout our car ride. He was desperately concentrating on the road. "So it can't restore the destroyed and damaged facilities to prewar levels."

Baghdad means the Garden of God. On the night of January 17 and for the forty-three days that followed, I watched CNN's live coverage of the SCUD missiles hitting Baghdad as the city slept, its breathing long, heavy, and patient. The coalition flew over 100,000 sorties and dropped on the city 88,500 tons of bombs, destroying military and civilian infrastructure which, in the words of a United Nations report, "pushed Iraq into a preindustrial age." Within moments the cradle of ancient civilization was reduced to piles of rubble.

The start of the Gulf War caused me to desperately miss Iraq. I began to think of Baghdad, and I wanted to re-experience the wonderful magic I experienced when, as a child, I walked to school in a custom-made uniform, my hair in braids, tied by bright white imitation silk ribbons. I remembered those walks so well: the frosty grass in the winter, birds chirping in spring, the sounds of my shoes click-clacking against an ancient surface that once was famed as the wealthiest and richest city in the world.

Baghdad was the center of learning and commerce where the House of Wisdom was built, imagine that. The House of Wisdom, a key institution in the translation movement where Greek, Persian, Sanskrit, Chinese and Syriac works were translated into Arabic and the concept of the library catalog was introduced. When the Mongol invaded Iraq in 1258, they destroyed the House of Wisdom along with all other libraries in Baghdad – the story of Iraq's life.

Given the media reports during the Gulf War, I felt Baghdad would soon be lost forever: 9,000 homes destroyed, along with the sole vaccine producing laboratory, all ports, eighty-three bridges, virtually all electrical power plants, oil refineries, oil storage facilities, electrically operated installations, plants manufacturing water treatment chemicals, postal systems, and telephone and communications systems. For months, we didn't know if my aunts, uncles, cousins, or my oldest sister and her five children were dead or alive.

The driver first dropped off Maysoon and her mother at their relatives' home. We arrived at my aunt's house around 3:30 am. My cousin Bushra opened the front door. Laughing and crying, she pulled me by the arm and hugged me with all her might. A heavy woman dressed in a floral nightgown, Bushra's hair was in disarray and half her teeth were missing. She wept into my shoulders and said she wanted to take in the scents of my mother and siblings whom she had not seen in twenty years. She recounted one-by-one all of my eleven siblings' names.

Raad and the driver brought my luggage into the gated front porch.

"I'll be in touch with you," Raad said. He gave me a paper with his telephone number. "And call me if you need anything."

My cousin thanked him profusely, they exchanged blessings, and she excitedly escorted me inside the living room, where the rest of the family was lined up to greet me. There was my Aunt Katina and her husband, Hikmat; her son, Bashar; and his wife, Zina. The young couple had a toddler boy and had been living with my aunt since they got married. There was also Bushra and her teenage children, who had come to spend the night in honor of my visit. The family members took turns welcoming me with a gentle hug or handshake and the traditional three kisses on the cheek — right, left, and right again — between relatives.

"You are tired," Aunt Katina said. "Come, I'll show you your bed."

Aunt Katina had a dark complexion and small black circles around her eyes. Her long braid was clipped in the back of her head. She had on a white nightgown with light colored prints. She resembled my mother, except she was taller and heavier set.

She opened the door to the family room. In the back corner was a bed set up for me. My cousin, Bashar, placed the luggage in my room and everyone bid me goodnight. I changed into a nightgown and lay on a bed with a thin mattress, a flat pillow, and a thin blanket. I stared at the ceiling and wondered why I had come here and whether I'd made a mistake by coming.

The sun was barely visible from the closed curtains, but it was enough for me to rush out of bed and go to the front porch without bothering to change from my nightgown or wear a robe. In Iraq it was customary for people to be out and about in their sleeping attire, as long as it was not lingerie. My aunt was already on the front porch, sweeping the cement floor.

"Good morning, Auntie."

"Good morning," she said. "It's only seven o'clock. Why are you up so early?"

"I always wake up early."

She sighed then went on sweeping. My aunt was a serious woman, like my mother. They had to be coerced into smiling, and they did not approve of too much laughter. I sat on the wide swing and listened to the birds chirp and the sound of her broom, made of palm tree fronds, swaying back and forth against the cement.

"Do you want tea?" she asked.

"Yes," I said, suddenly realizing that I would have to do without American coffee for the next three and a half weeks.

She went inside, and her toddler grandson peeked outside the front door. When he saw me, he shyly hid behind the wall. A minute later his shyness was gone and he was playing in the dirt of the small plant and tree garden in the corner of the house.

"Cicko! Don't touch the plants!" she yelled at him. Cicko was his nickname.

"Auntie, why don't you let him go outside?" I asked, looking at the walled fence and gated door that closed off the front yard from the street.

"Outside where?"

"On the street."

"The street!" she gasped. "What would he do out in the streets?"

"Play."

Her eyes gazed down and traveled far. She parked the broomstick in her palms and lightly leaned against it. With the absence of her sweeping, the chirping of birds grew louder. She took a deep breath. "Oh daughter, gone are those days. Gone are those days."

A sad breeze swept over me. In the 1970s children owned the streets during the hours when they were not in school. We were like the train gate in control of traffic. When a car drove by, we scattered left and right to make way, and once the car passed, we resumed playing jump rope, hopscotch, tag, hide-and-go-seek, and the all-time favorite, marbles, where we drew a circle on the ground with a stick, placed all the marbles in the circle, then shot their smooth and brightly colored glass sphere to knock the other marbles out of the circle.

We did not worry about thieves or kidnappers because the majority of mothers stayed at home and watched the children, theirs and the whole neighborhoods', as if they had binoculars implanted on all sides of their heads. We didn't have toys, board games, or electronic games. Television programming started at 6 pm, opening up with Quranic prayers, then children's shows, followed by regular family programming, and the news. By midnight, the screen would go dark and then the colored bars came on, followed by the pink noise and static-filled screen. In the summer, two additional hours of programming were added in the morning to get the kids out of their mother's hair. Our district was our amusement park. We didn't need waterslides, merry-go-rounds, Ferris wheels, roller coasters, cotton candy, popcorn, and lemonade. We just had a simple desire to be together and to be creative.

Once the early morning winter frosts had given way to spring, the wild flowers and fruit trees sprouted over the land the way in which brown and yellow grass turned green here in America. There are more than 3,300 plants and flowers in Iraq. The scent of palm trees, fig trees, citrus trees, berries, jasmine, sunflowers, and roses, the national flower of Iraq and the United States, is enough to cure ailments and feed the soul before their parts are removed and used for food or traditional medicine.

In the summer our bedrooms were dismantled and our pillows, bed sheets, and blankets were carried to the rooftop, where they were set up in rows so we could sleep under an open sky. The rooftop was a real entertainment. During broad daylight, we would go to the rooftop and watch the man in a white tank top smoke, his arms resting over the roofless wall; a woman hang bed sheets, pajamas, nightgowns, and men's tank tops and pants on a clothesline; our neighbor's older sister hold up a mirror in a well-lit corner as she plucked her eyebrows; a young student across the street who liked to pace back and forth while reading his book.

In the falling twilight we would crawl out of our beds on the rooftops to chase after the moon that changed direction whenever we changed direction. We'd stand on top of the beds, raise our voice, and call out to our friends next door, asking them, "What are you doing?" Or we argued about who the moon was actually following, us or them, until our mothers would hush us up and scuttle us back to bed. Lovers had their own secret way of utilizing the rooftop, which we were then too young to learn the details of.

Every July 14, we watched the fireworks celebrating the 1958 revolution that took place in Iraq, marking the overthrow of the Hashemite monarchy established by King Faisal in 1932 under the support of the British. One July 14, as we competed with the neighbors across our roof, we screamed so loud and jumped so hard that the bed broke and we fell through to the ground. The neighbors laughed hysterically and we got up, all red-faced.

"Yes, very nice," my mother had said back in Michigan when I was dreaming out loud about returning to my birth country. "Sleeping on the rooftop and being woken up first thing in the morning with a spoonful of flies in your mouth."

"The occasional fly," – or two, or three, or ten – "never bothered me," I lied.

Yes, the rooftop was real entertainment.

"Auntie, when will you set up the beds on the rooftop this year?" I asked.

She looked at me like I was out of my mind. "Daughter, no one sleeps on the rooftop anymore!"

"What? Why?"

"It's dangerous."

"Dangerous?"

I had not been awake for more than an hour and already the Baghdad I knew had a different tone than the Baghdad I grew up in. Since the 1991 Gulf War, the thugs that were otherwise petrified of Saddam let themselves loose. The Iraqi government was able to take control of the city within a short time, but could not return it to the prewar safety standards. After the outbreak of the war, when looting was at its highest, entering a house through the rooftop seemed less risky to thieves and criminals than breaking through the windows or front door, where they might be seen by neighbors. At the rooftop, criminals reasoned, the owners of the house could be held at knife point and then forced to go into the house and reveal their stash of gold and money. Yet some feared the rooftop for another reason. They worried that if they slept there, they would not hear the burglars break in through the window or front door. These unsettling thoughts brought many frightening thoughts to Iraqis, so I discovered from day one that the rooftop was a definite no, no.

"Cheer up, Weam. You are actually seeing the better days of Iraq," my cousins said with a smile when they saw my disappointment about how much Iraq had changed since I left in 1980.

During the Gulf War and the time period prior to the UN Security Council implementing the Oil-for-Food program in 1996, Iraq suffered a worse state. Ice cream, candy, and soda factories were all shut down because there wasn't enough sugar to go around, and restaurants were forbidden from cooking meat, only vegetarian dishes, like burgul. Bread was made from barley, flour, crushed fava beans, and palm date pits and had a chocolate coloring. Children called it "cocoa bread."

"How did it taste?" I'd once asked my husband, who'd lived through the sanctions.

"It was bread," he said. "The most important thing was for people to be full, not to go to sleep starving."

Bakeries were not allowed to bake white bread, and people started making their own tanoor oven at home. They bought flour and sugar from the black market and baked their own bread. The Iraqi government made a rations system, a food basket, which continued throughout the sanctions, allowing each Iraqi citizen a monthly allowance of wheat, sugar, salt, cooking oil, tea, soap, and sometimes one whole frozen chicken.

"Saddam eats deer meat and Iraqi people eat date pits," Iraqis would say about the sanctions. Some Muslim Iraqis began to call Christian Iraqis "Bush's people" and grew to dislike them for that reason. They felt that Saddam, by finding ways to feed them, had rescued them from Bush's attempt to starve them. They were also not too fond of Bush emptying their clinics and hospitals of medicine and proper working equipment, polluting their water, and crushing their telephone and electricity system.

"Katina!" my aunt's husband bellowed from inside the house. She set the broom against the wall and went to see what he wanted.

Bashar, who was a few years older than me, came outside in his pajamas. He bid me good morning and sat beside me on the swing. The last I remembered of Bashar was when he'd tried to stuff dirty socks in my nose and mouth when I was a little girl. He was also famous for going around telling everyone that he could whistle through his ear. "Show us," my brothers had said to him.

He pulled on his earlobe as he whistled through his mouth. "See?" he said. They slapped the back of his neck and laughed uncontrollably.

Bashar was now a grown man with a moustache, a wife, and a child. But I noticed by the way his mother glanced reproachfully at him each time he tried to carry a conversation that he was not considered quite grown up yet, not by her standards. Bashar worked full-time as a mechanic for three dollars a month.

"Is that enough for a family to live on?" I asked.

He cracked up, covering his mouth and slightly hiding his head as though not to embarrass me for asking such a ridiculous question. "My aunt sends us money from America. I work just to have something to do."

The Christian population was a lot wealthier than Muslims because they had relatives outside of Iraq living in the United States, Europe, and Australia who regularly sent money.

"You need to get dressed and go get kabob from down the street," his mother said as she parked the broom at the edge of the wall.

"Oh, can I go too?" I asked.

"Sure," Bashar said, all smiles.

His mother gave him a deadly look. "It's not safe for her to walk in the streets. What if something were to happen?"

He stood defeated. I was stunned at how quickly he gave in and decided I would fend for myself. "Auntie, I must go for a walk," I said. "I've been traveling for nearly two days. My legs are stiff and in pain. Besides, at home, I'm used to taking long walks every day."

She was perplexed. She gave him one more deadly look as if to say that this was his fault. "Just to the kabob stand and back!" she warned.

I went inside and ran into my aunt's husband. He was a tall man with a big stomach and skinny legs that showed through his wide shorts. I greeted him and went into the room to change. Someone opened the door before I even removed my slippers. It was my aunt and Zina, Bashar's wife. Zina was in her early twenties, a pretty girl with full lips, fair skin, and long, curly hair.

"Give me all your money, passport, and whatever valuables you have," Zina said.

"She will keep it safe for you," my aunt said.

I turned over my little pouch of $3,000, my passport,

and my driver's license. They exited the room, and I put on a tight short sleeved shirt over my long flaring skirt and open toe sandals. The weather was warm and sunny, the type we only had in Michigan during summertime.

Bashar and I headed out. The main road was a block away. There were rows of shops, restaurants, sidewalk stores, and vending carts. The area was energized with the smell of cigarettes, fumes, dust, grilled kabobs, and hot cardamom tea. Merchants shouted out the products or services they were selling, like purses and shoe shining, while drivers beeped their horns.

"*Sabaah al-khayr*," my cousin said as he greeted some people along the way with a quick salute.

Two young women carrying books passed us. They were college students and the only girls I had seen on the street wearing a head scarf that covered their hair.

"Women here don't veil much, do they?" I asked, trying to keep up with Bashar. He was not walking fast, but I was busy taking everything in: the clothes hanging on top of the shops, the fresh juice bars serving pomegranate juice, the donkey pulling a wagon filled with gas tanks.

"No, Saddam wants to keep them westernized," Bashar said. He stopped at a curb of a busy street, extended his arm in front of me, and looked both ways. He put his arm down and motioned for me to cross. "Saddam is against the Muslim Brotherhood. If a woman is caught veiling from head to toe, where even her face is covered, she will be killed and thrown in the street as an example for other women not to do the same."

No wonder no one in the street batted an eye at me

for wearing western clothes. "In Jordan, a lot of women are veiled from head to toe," I said.

"Oh, well, the Muslim Brotherhood has been in Jordan for a long time. They got strong, especially after the Gulf War."

We returned home with a tray of kabob and a bag of fresh, hot bread. Bashar was reprimanded for taking a long time. My aunt's other daughter, Zikra, had come over with her young children. She sat on the couch, breastfeeding her baby.

"Your cousins will come to see you later today," my aunt said to me. "Have all their gifts and money ready so you can distribute it accordingly."

I went into the room to change. There was a knock, and the door opened before I gave anyone permission to enter. I was half naked. "Can I have a word with you?" Zikra asked.

She was in my face, bouncing her baby on her waist before I could answer. And that was pretty much the way it went for the remainder of the trip. I was bombarded by female relatives who found it easiest to catch me alone when I changed clothes. They wanted me to know all their business and serve as a mediator for their family dramas or be a messenger for their relatives in the United States. Their requests were pretty similar, with very slight variations, and went something like this:

"Can you tell my brother or sister or aunt or uncle or niece or nephew or cousin or in-laws to send me fifty dollars a month? My husband doesn't work, and what difference would it make if he did work since three dollars of a monthly salary can't support a cockroach or an ant or a fly or a spider or a moth. With fifty dollars, I can buy eggs, meat, milk, and

70

during Easter and Christmas, clothes for the children, and I could even put a little on the side, in case of an emergency, God forbid. Rumor has it that my relatives live a very good life in America, that to them fifty dollars is nothing, it's like a couple of bucks. They spend fifty dollars per person when they eat out at a restaurant, and not a very fancy restaurant at that. And if my relatives think fifty dollars is too much to ask, then they can combine their efforts to help. That way, individual families would not have to carry the fifty dollar burden alone."

In the evenings, my aunt's family and I received some of our visitors in semi-darkness, as the sun was still on the horizon but the electricity was down. Those who came at night were greeted with flashlights and candle lights. Prior to the Gulf War, the total installed generating capacity was 9,295 megawatts with a peak demand of about 5,100 megawatts. Approximately 87 percent of Iraq's population had access to electricity. The war had, however, severely damaged the entire power system infrastructure in Iraq, and so electricity was generally shut off. The Iraqi government was eventually able to arrange a system where cities alternated the electricity's usage so that Baghdad would have electricity for three hours, then Basra for three hours, then Fallujah, and so on. Some people who had generators were able to avoid the power outages. The good news was that in those days, electricity was free of charge. Water was free as well, except it was only clean in Baghdad and other cities in the north, not in the south, where water had to be boiled before drinking because the importation of chlorine was embargoed by sanctions.

A document from the Defense Intelligence Agency dated January 22, 1991, addressed the possible countermeasures to obtain drinkable water despite sanctions:

> Iraq conceivably could truck water from the mountain reservoirs to urban areas. But the capability to gain significant quantities is extremely limited. The amount of pipe on hand and the lack of pumping stations would limit laying pipelines to these reservoirs. Moreover, without chlorine purification, the water still would contain biological pollutants. Some affluent Iraqis could obtain their own minimally adequate supply of good quality water from northern Iraqi sources. If boiled, the water could be safely consumed. Poorer Iraqis and industries requiring large quantities of pure water would not be able to meet their needs.

Meaning men, women, and children had to bathe and wash clothes and kitchen utensils in water contaminated with raw sewage, which they did.

* * *

Between barbecuing, canoeing, hiking, and changing diapers, I could not finish reading the entire transcripts during our Labor Day weekend family trip, but I had read enough to know that the court had wasted its time and taxpayer money with the wrong persons. Dawn and Darrin Hanna did not commit an act harmful to an individual, community, or the state. The people that should have been tried and convicted were those who not only bombed Iraq, mercilessly and repeatedly, but who slowly tortured it by playing God and depriving its citizens of the smallest necessities.

The wars and sanctions were the crimes, the real honest-to-goodness crimes, crimes which ought to have had punishable consequences, not permitted to continue their criminal pattern by, in the name of "national security," locking up or sending off to war ordinary American citizens and destroying families.

CHAPTER 7
The Disfavors Handed to Us

When we arrived home from Cran-Hill Ranch, I hurriedly bathed the kids then prepared a light dinner of cucumber yogurt salad, pre-packed hummus dip, and kettle potato chips, which Iraqis called "Iraqi chips" because it resembled the kind made and sold in Iraq. Potato chips cooked in a pot on a stove at home are technically kettle chips, and in the olden days, Iraqi vendors sold them fresh from a street cart by scooping them from a container and into a small paper bag.

My husband watched and fed the kids as I unpacked. Once I was done, I made a cup of coffee and right at nine o'clock, grabbed the remote control, jumped on the couch, and switched the channel from Al Iraqia news to the Bravo Channel. *The Real Housewives of New Jersey* were having their season finale reunion.

"Didn't they already show this?" my husband asked.

"No."

"They're wearing the same clothes; it's the same set."

"The other was part one of the reunion. This is part two."

This was my one and only favorite show and serious addiction, except for coffee. Little by little, and thanks to me, or no thanks to me, the show began to grow on my husband, the same way his news channels and sports games sometimes grew on me. When commercial break came, I lowered the TV volume.

"I want to work on the Dawn Hanna story," I said. "Maybe do a documentary."

"It is an interesting story," he said, dipping the chips in the hummus and then handing it to my daughter. "And you would be doing a humanitarian thing."

"Yes, but those are not my only reasons," I said in Arabic, the language I used with family when I had something deep to say. "When the 2003 war broke out, there was so much I had to say, that I wanted to say, but I felt that the American public did not like hearing my version of the story."

I had done many radio interviews for my first book, which came out a year after the war, and there were callers, once or twice even the host, who were upset at me for simply telling them my experience of growing up in Iraq in the 1970s and visiting that country in 2000. The harshest audiences were from the stations in the South. They thought they knew Iraq, Saddam, Islam, and the situation there better than I did. They expected me to say that I had a miserable childhood and to clap and cheer for all the hurt done on Iraq and for our troops sacrificing their lives for a great cause. One woman from my writer's group got really upset that I wasn't *grateful* for what the United States was doing for the people of Iraq.

I quickly realized that it was discomforting for many to hear anything contrary to what the media was telling them, especially from a girl of Iraqi origin, so I began to lock my words and thoughts in my throat.

I picked a few chips off the floor. "I feel that through this case, I can say everything I've been holding in for the past nineteen years."

"That's not the important point, Weam," he said, continuing to feed my daughter. "The important point is can your project help her?"

"What do you mean that's not an important point!" I dashed to the kitchen and returned with a wet rag to wipe the hummus off the table. "That is a very important point."

The *Housewives* were back on. I hushed everyone and faced the television set. Keeping in mind that my husband had a bachelor's degree in statistics and bookkeeping, I tried not to be overly angry at him.

I waited for the next commercial break to speak to him again. "Yes, I think this project can help her," I said. "If it doesn't release her from prison, at least it could exonerate her name. That will make a difference for her in the future, when she's out."

"Then go ahead and do it, if it's for a humanitarian cause."

"What about that other thing?"

"What other thing?"

I stared at him. He knew what I was talking about, but either he was trying to remain strong or, like me, trying to ignore what happened not long ago between us and Homeland

Security. In 2003, the US Immigration and Naturalization Service (INS) ceased to exist, and its service and benefit functions were transferred to the newly created US Citizenship and Immigration Services (USCIS) within the Department of Homeland Security (DHS). They implemented policies that caused delays and uncomfortable tactics, such as profiling, in the naturalization process. These policies troubled my home as we waited and waited for my husband's immigration papers to process.

"You think immigration won't process my immigration papers if you do a story about Dawn?" he asked.

I shrugged.

"Weam, if you do it, do it for *Allah*," he said. "Maybe He'll bless us."

Allah is derived from the Chaldean word *Allaha*. The word is older than Judaism, Christianity, and Islam. Arabic speakers of all Abrahamic faiths use the word *Allah* to mean "God," and they use it often throughout the day, as often as we here say words such as "like" or "I mean." In the Hebrew and Chaldea dictionary of the Old Testament, the word *Allah* is described as, "To go up; ascend; climb."

There are many disputes about the origin of the word and its meaning. The bottom line is while God's name can be changed, the rules are the same. If you do bad, bad will happen to you or your children. If you do good, good will happen to you or your children. If something important was calling out for your attention and you ignored it, you were ignoring a calling from God, *Allaha*, the Universe, the Great Spirit, or whatever name is placed on this sacred energy. Then you will have to deal with its weight on your conscience. My husband was obviously more afraid of karma than he was of the government. Me? I wanted to express myself and provide a service. With regards to Dawn Hanna, perhaps I would finally be allowed to speak my truth and to combine writing with a service to a woman, and my specialty, to a family.

Once my show was over, my husband switched the channel to Al Iraqiya, and I went on my computer to check my emails. I had an email from a producer in LA of Middle Eastern origin whom I'll call Issa. Issa was working on a documentary called *The Prosecution of George W. Bush for Murder*, written by and starring Vincent Bugliosi. Bugliosi was famous for prosecuting Charles Manson and later wrote a book about the case, *Helter Skelter*. The documentary about prosecuting Bush was based on Bugliosi's book.

Issa emailed me a link to a televised interview with Richard Fine, a seventy-year-old attorney who was never convicted of a crime but yet was held in solitary confinement in Central Men's jail for more than a year, as punishment inflicted by an LA superior judge. His crime was exposing the corrupt practices of the California judges, the Sheriff, and the County. I watched bits of the interview where Fine cited the tremendous cost to the California taxpayers of hundreds of millions of dollars over the last two decades. Judges were paid under the table while standing for election to their offices every six years. He also warned that America, whose citizens had fought for independence from the king of England, had now returned to a country without a functioning justice system, a country that had undermined the essence of the democratic process. Seeing this case's similarity to Dawn's, I called Issa for advice.

"How is the documentary about Bush going?" I asked.

He sighed heavily. "I've turned over every rock trying to get this film finished, but no one person or group is willing to put their money where their mouth is. You know, when I first heard of this project, I thought it would be received with cheers and cash. The only thing I've seen so far is crickets."

"Is there anything I can do to help?"

"Well, I'm coming to the Dearborn area sometime soon and I was thinking, hoping, that maybe you might know of any organizations or individuals there that might consider investing $50,000. If you know of anyone, that would be great! No worries if you don't."

"I can introduce you to a couple of people," I said.

"Ahhh, thank you very much, Weam!" Issa had a deep voice, and when he spoke, he dramatized everything with his slow and extreme way of expressing his thoughts.

"Issa, I've been researching a case that I feel is very important, the Dawn Hanna case. I want to make a documentary about it for now and possibly a book in the future. I'm hoping you can give me a few pointers."

"Why don't you send me the link to Dawn's website and call me tomorrow?"

After we hung up, I checked my inbox. Linda had sent nine emails over Labor Day weekend. The first e-mail contained a visitor form to fill out so I could visit Dawn in prison. The others had links to articles about Najib Shemami, Dawn's uncle; affidavits sent by the two CIA operatives; a thirty-page questionnaire submission that Barbara Mc-Quade, Dawn's prosecutor, filled out to apply for the Detroit

Attorney General position, which she now holds. In the application, McQuade was asked to cite the ten most significant litigated matters that she handled. She cited Dawn Hanna's case as her number one case and Dawn's uncle's case, Najib, as her number two case.

McQuade's interest in government could be traced back to her days as a reporter for *The Daily*, during which time her favorite book was *All the President's Men*, a story about two journalists who'd investigated President Richard Nixon's Watergate scandal. "What reporters and prosecutors do is very similar," she'd once said in an interview. "Looking for wrongdoing and looking for misconduct and trying to expose that. I think that influence certainly inspired me to do what I do today."

There was also a link to an article about US General Attorney Eric Holder's speech on November 19, 2009, to Arab Americans and Muslims, telling them that their full rights must be protected as America battled security threats. He said:

> For the last nine months, I've heard from Muslim and Arab Americans who feel uneasy about their relationship with their government, who feel isolated and discriminated against by law enforcement. It is inconsistent with what America is all about....This is not blind adherence to political correctness. It is devotion to our founding documents.

There was a letter to Judge Marianne O. Battani, who

sentenced Dawn, from Fred, a man in DC who was an active army counterintelligence worker for over thirty years. He implored the Judge to review Dawn Hanna's case and told her that Emad, the CIA operative, contacted him and confided that he was very perplexed that such a prosecution could take place in the United States. Fred wrote:

> It seemed to Emad that the prosecution meshed unrelated business queries and transactions into a larger conspiracy that simply did not exist. When Emad saw what had happened to Dawn, he offered to fly to the United States and testify in any forum to ensure her release from prison for her unwitting participation in his support to a CIA operation.

Fred told the Judge that from the limited research he had done, it appeared that Emad was well-known to the US Government and participated in helping them overthrow Saddam Hussein and establish a new government in Iraq. He wrote:

> From a national perspective, the case may have a chilling effect on persons cooperating with our country around the world. When sensitive sources lack confidence that the US Government will protect them and their activities, likely fewer will put themselves and their interests at risk to support its agencies.

Ms. Hanna's sentence for a simple customs violation seems grossly excessive. The determination with which US Government agencies pursued this alleged customs violation, suppressed information from the defense, and then sought such a lengthy prison term could lead some to question whether Ms. Hanna's Arab ethnicity in the post-9/11 environment pushed this case to be treated differently than other alleged customs violations. I think this case warrants congressional review to determine whether current laws and policies are sufficient to ensure adequate protections of US Citizens and access to sufficient information to mount a viable defense.

This same letter was sent to various government officials. Within nine days, Fred received a letter stating that Judge Battani will not read an *ex parte* communication on a case before her. She asked Fred to forward his letter to the attorneys for both the government and Ms. Hanna and thanked him for taking the time to communicate about a matter in which, she wrote, "you apparently have an interest or information."

Fred was outraged and wrote back:

I am surprised and disappointed that, in spite of having new and specific information that supports Ms. Hanna's claim of innocence, the

> US Justice System has not intervened to ensure justice – even if it might be embarrassing to the US Government. Hiding information from the defense and jury is inconsistent with the US Constitution and legal precedence. This apparent injustice is so egregious that several people have placed their lives and livelihoods at risk to expose their affiliation with our government's activities.

Although I wanted to spew this bitter subject out of my head, I was hooked. I googled Dawn Hanna's name and found reports that Dawn wanted to delay her sentence by two weeks in order to freeze her eggs before going to prison due to her age, thirty-six, and the length of the sentence, six years. The Judge refused, saying that Dawn had plenty of time to get her personal business in order.

People posted online the following in the comments box: *Just have her move the eggs near her cold heart and they'll be fine; Great! She wants to produce more little crooks?; Thanks judge – you did her future offspring and the general public a big favor.*

Some favor.

The United States has the highest incarceration rate in the world, with the population of inmates housed in prisons and jails exceeding two million, a 500 percent increase over the past thirty years. Half of all persons incarcerated under state jurisdiction are for non-violent offenses, and 20 percent are incarcerated for drug offenses. The length of time served in prison has increased strikingly over the last two decades. Many prisons are overcrowded, and so every year, over ten counties consider building new jails. In July 2010, for instance, Lubbock County officials commemorated the opening of the new Lubbock County Detention Center with a ribbon-cutting ceremony and guided tours of the 400,000-square-foot $110 million facility.

No, a favor was not the proper word to describe Dawn's incarceration. It was more like a disfavor, so sugarcoated that it was tough for the palate of an inexperienced chef to recognize its true ingredient.

CHAPTER 8
Take This Case at Your Own Risk

The phone rang, and the caller ID said "Unknown Caller." I was inside my daughter's classroom, where the teacher was reading a book called *The Kissing Hand*. It was my daughter's first day of preschool. The children sat on the oval rug, their necks stretched up high as they listened. They looked like ducklings with their mother duck. My son played in the toy kitchen area. He picked up a skillet and put inside it a plastic egg that was sunny-side up.

"Watch my son for a minute," I told my sister-in-law. It was her daughter's first day of school as well.

I stepped out into the hallway and answered the phone. An automated message came on. "You have a prepaid call from an inmate at a federal prison. To accept this call, press five. To decline, hang up. If you do not wish to receive any future calls from this inmate, press seven."

I pressed five. "Hi, Dawn."

"Hi, Weam. Are you busy?"

"I'm at my daughter's school. It's her first day."

"Thanks for taking my call."

"No problem," I said, knowing she had to wait a while in line to make her calls. "So, how is everything?"

"It's okay, I guess. Just tired of waiting every day for something to happen and then nothing gets done. Everyone knows this is a grave injustice, but yet they can do nothing about it. I continue to sit here and suffer mentally and physically day after day after day."

For almost a week, Dawn and I had been corresponding regularly. She added my name to her list of phone contacts, and I signed up to Corrlink, the official email system used by the Bureau of Prisons to allow inmates to communicate with the outside world. It is a fee-based system - $0.15 per minute and $0.15 per printed page of messages – that inmates must pay for in order to send or receive email. In many US federal prisons, inmate wages start at 12 cents per hour.

In the first few days of our communications, Dawn seemed to be a good trooper about her prison life. Soon the side of her that kept Darrin away appeared from behind closed curtains, and I saw how she was like a prop in the hands of a magician. One minute she was a shivering kitten left out in the freezing rain; the other minute she was a hungry wolf, drooling to grab its prey, its freedom, by the teeth and devour it.

Darrin described it best when he said, "Dawn is like a lamb in a well, everyday screaming and screaming and screaming. It's heartbreaking. And it's so hard to get that lamb out, to get justice served, when there's this screaming, this piercing scream, of what sounds like a lamb in a grinder in a well."

"How did Darrin's meeting go in Washington?" I asked Dawn in order to change the subject. "Ron Scott went with him, didn't he?"

"Yes, but I don't believe anybody anymore," she said. "Ron Scott comes from the same brood of people that told my family I would be home last Christmas, one day was too much for this girl to be in prison, injustice has been done, civil rights violated, yadda yadda. Everything is 'Soon!' 'Sit tight!' 'People in power are working on it!' I appreciate the efforts, but until I am free and the nightmare is over, this is all lip service."

"Ron is speaking at an Amnesty conference coming up. He'll be mentioning your case to the audience, and I heard he'll also approach Amnesty members to take on this case. They take cases that violate human rights, especially those in which one case will have an impact for many others – where a difference can be made."

"When is the conference?" she asked, her voice softening.

"It's soon. I'm not sure the dates. I'd have to check with your mom."

She was quiet. "Have you called Emad yet?"

"I called yesterday and a woman answered, said Emad was coming back in half an hour."

"That's either his wife or her mother."

"By the time I was able to call back, it was late at night there. I think they're six hours ahead of us."

"Will you call him today?"

"I should be able to. My daughter's class is almost over and the only major thing I have to do when I get home is make dolma."

"Oh my God, don't say that! Dolma!"

"Oops! Sorry."

"My favorite!" she cried, then called me a few indecent names. "I hate you! I'll be dreaming about the dolma tonight while I eat my expired, nasty food."

"They feed you expired food?"

She laughed. "Are you serious? The produce here is generally spoiled. We have to pick off the rotten lettuce from the bunch, and the fruit, like apples and oranges, are half frozen. The meat is gray and the canned foods are defects, expired, seconds, or about to turn."

"You have one minute remaining," an automated voice said.

"If I end up choking on my dolma, I'll assume it's because of you," I said. "I'll be sure to first smudge the pot with sage to ward off the evil spirits."

We laughed.

"Yeah, I'll try not to think of you eating dolma while I eat food that's marked 'not fit for human consumption.'"

"Hey, if it was good enough for the Iraqis during the sanctions, it's good enough for you."

In 1995, Bill Clinton introduced the Oil-for-Food program which, through a UN- managed escrow account, permitted Iraq to export some oil and raise money to import food, medicine, and certain civilian humanitarian items. Under the program, the UN authorized the shipments of an extensive list of items, including telecommunications equip-

88

ment. While the program did ease the tightness of the sanctions, it suffered from widespread corruption and abuse. A $34 million UN-appointed panel, led by Paul Volcker, published a 623-page report on its investigation into the scandal. The report documented a huge amount of evidence regarding manipulation of the $60 billion Oil-for-Food program by the Saddam Hussein regime with the collaboration of more than 2,200 companies in 66 countries as well as a number of prominent international politicians. Volcker stated that much of the food aid supplied under the program "was unfit for human consumption" and that it was UN mismanagement and failure of the world's most powerful nations to end corruption in the program that "allowed Saddam to fill his coffers."

Once the fifteen-minute call ended, I returned to the classroom in time to help my daughter make a kissing hand with an imprint of her hand on paper.

My niece Dena stopped by with treats for my kids in the afternoon. I took advantage of the few moments of Dena giving my kids treats to stuff the vegetables and grape leaves for the pot of dolma I planned to cook the next day.

"Deday is her attorney?" Dena asked, glancing at the transcripts on the coffee table.

"You've heard of him?"

"He's one of the best attorneys in Michigan. We studied him in law school."

I was surprised.

"He's really crazy, in an amazing way. The way he questions and re-examines a witness makes you dizzy, like you wonder, what the hell just happened?"

"I had gotten too dizzy reading the transcripts all right, but it was because a lot of it was incredibly boring," I said as I finished scooping the flesh of the eggplants and started on the zucchini. She kept staring at Deday's name on the transcripts.

"I can't believe that Deday wasn't able to get her acquitted," she said. "Or at least get a lower sentence."

Deday LaRene is a Jewish man who Dawn said "resembled a mini Albert Einstein" with his small frame and slightly long white hair that looked like cotton. She had met with almost every attorney in Detroit who did federal work and ended up hiring LaRene because he had an excellent reputation and was said to know the law off the top of his head.

"Can you take the kids out to the playground while I make a quick phone call?" I asked.

"Yeah, yeah, go ahead."

"It's an important overseas call and it'll be hard to focus with background noise…"

"Don't worry about it."

I washed and dried my hands, searched my purse for a calling card, and grabbed a pen and notebook. I called Emad. After he picked up, I introduced myself and my intention of doing a documentary about Dawn's case. "I'd like to know whether you are willing to be interviewed, because to be honest, without your side of the story, we have no story."

"Anything to fix this injustice," he said in his British-Arab accent. "This is an injustice by purpose, not by mistake. That's exactly what used to happen in Iraq and other dictatorship countries."

"Why do you think the government refuses to release Dawn?"

"I have no idea. It's beyond one's imagination that this is taking place, especially in America, the land of the free. I wrote a letter to the Judge, but no one is listening to me even though I have first-hand knowledge of what happened."

I remembered the times people did not want to listen to me after the 2003 war.

"Dawn didn't technically do anything wrong," he said. "All she did is trust me, and I didn't tell the whole truth. Initially, they should remove restrictions on a lot of the government documents."

"They're saying there's a national threat associated with this information."

"She is not a threat, so why are they being restricted?"

Eight months prior to trial, on January 24, 2008, the government filed a Motion for Protective Order, invoking the Classified Information Procedures Act (CIPA) and requesting the non-disclosure of certain allegedly classified information. CIPA was passed in 1980, and its primary purpose was to limit the practice of graymail by criminal defendants in possession of sensitive government secrets. "Graymail" refers to the threat by a criminal defendant to disclose classified information during the course of a trial. The graymail defendant essentially presented the government with a "Hobson's choice": either allow disclosure of the classified information or dismiss the indictment. CIPA was not intended to infringe on a defendant's right to a fair trial or to change the existing rules of evidence in criminal procedure.

In the Hanna case, the government sought, and was

granted, an *ex parte, in camera* hearing to review the evidence at issue. An *ex parte* judicial proceeding is conducted for the benefit of only one party. *In camera* means in private. *Ex parte, in camera* hearings are a closed and private court session. The public galleries are cleared, the doors are locked, and the only people in attendance are the Judge, the court reporter, and the parties involved, which in this case was just the government. At no time did the defendants receive any information regarding the contents of the withheld evidence.

Ex parte, in camera hearings are harshly limited by the Fifth and Fourteenth Amendments, which state that a person shall not be deprived of any interest in liberty or property without due process of law. It is a rare and infrequent occurrence for a court to grant something like this because public access and transparency are both paramount to justice. Not so since 9/11. Six weeks after the September 11 attacks, US Congress enacted the USA Patriot Act that was signed into law by President George W. Bush. Treating all US citizens as enemies of the state, the act allowed court proceedings to be held in secret and *ex parte* at the request of the government.

I looked at the backyard through our glass doors. My niece had my son on her lap as she pushed my daughter on the swing. I called Issa. After dialing his number, I cradled the phone between my neck and shoulder and pealed three onions, cut the very top and bottom of each, and made a cut down one side of each onion.

"Weam, they just released Richard Fine," he said, his voice full of excitement and suspense. "This is a powerful statement. It says, in the end, we the people do have a say in how the justice system is run!"

"Wow, that's great news," I said, and we discussed Richard Fine for a bit before he said, "By the way, I had a chance to review Dawn's case and I have a whole lot of questions!"

I asked Issa if it was okay that, during our conversation, I would be working in the kitchen. He would likely hear the faucet running, the clutter and clatter of pots, dishes and utensils, and he said, "By all means, do what you have to do!" I thanked him, but before I had gotten his consent, I had started filling a pot with water, enough to cover the onions by one inch. Once boiled, onion layers soften and separate easily.

"So, the incriminating emails," he said. "Those are my main concern because they obviously convince the jurors that Dawn is guilty. These emails are a bit racy, don't you think? They show that Dawn is far from being a Mother Theresa."

"Well, we're all far from that."

"True, true. But you are telling a story here that must rise to the occasion and put the people who have done wrong behind bars, so you must address these emails where Dawn contacts different vendors telling them that she wants to skirt around Iraq to get items into Iraq."

Actually, I did not want to put anyone behind bars. I did not tell him that, but I told him what Dawn told me. The government wanted a plea bargain of four to five years. Dawn and Darrin had two separate attorneys who both felt that that was not much of a deal and strongly suggested that this case go to trial. Afterward, the discovery from the government started coming in: boxes full of five years' worth of bank documents, 15,000 emails on CD ROM, and hard copy documents seized from the search warrant at the office. Dawn and Darrin went through every page individually and then together in some cases. They noticed that the emails that were considered evidence were random emails that were not in proper order so that someone looking at it could not see the whole thread of a conversation. For instance, an email from April of 2002 was put next to an email from January of 2002. Dawn told her brother, "Look at this! They're going to take all the different deals I was working on, shuffle things up, and lump them together to show a story they want to create."

"Basically, they were going to edit the story to fit their needs," Issa said.

I filled another pot with water to boil the cabbage leaves I had cut earlier from the head roll. This softened the cabbage so I could easily roll it. I said, "Darrin ended up writing a program for the lawyers that was a customized database for searching documents by date, time, to and from, and then he made it quite advanced with a filter where one could search by keywords, like Emad + Telecom + Iraq and > 2001."

"So they *were* working on deals for Iraq?"

"They were trying to. At first, Dawn thought that the telecom was permitted into Iraq through the Oil-for-Food program. It was, but you had to first get a license because certain parts of the telecommunications equipment had crypto-graph-ic capabilities." I had difficulty pronouncing the word even though I was reading it off index notes I had on top of the kitchen counter, next to the grape leaves.

For over a decade there have been many reports that say that cryptography is not a weapon and that the British and US Government have failed to present a credible case to justify export controls on cryptography. Cryptography is the art of secret writing, originally invented by regular people to protect commerce and, as is suggested in *Kama Sutra*, hide secret romances.

The earliest forms of cryptography required little more than writing tools since most people could not read. The first recorded instance of a cryptographic technique was written by an Egyptian scribe on stone almost four millennia ago. The second is a Mesopotamian tablet containing an enciphered formula for the making of glazes for pottery. In more modern eras, encryption was used in an attempt to ensure secrecy in communication between spies, military leaders, and diplomats. Julius Caesar, Mary, Queen of Scots, and Hitler used it.

In recent decades, cryptography has expanded due to a number of factors, one major one being the Internet. In his essay, "Cryptography Timeline," Carl Ellison wrote, "The invention of cryptography is not limited to either civilians or the government. Wherever the need for secrecy is felt, the invention occurs."

Three people assured Dawn that she could easily get the license for the telecommunication equipment under the Oil-for-Food program, but that she first had to get a quote from vendors. One was her father, who was working at the time as a contractor in Iraq for the US Army – although during the trial, he was regularly referred to as a store owner. Another person was Saed Barzani, a business colleague who became Dawn's close friend and advisor.

Barzani is an Iraqi Kurd with US citizenship who lived in Virginia and had strong ties to the Iraqi and US government. And there was Emad, who had strong government ties in numerous places. After Saddam was toppled, Emad's cousin became the first interim president of Iraq. Emad was even asked to take a political position in Iraq, but he refused.

"So this CIA guy is big-time," Issa said.

"Obviously, and the telecom was a $27 million deal. When Dawn was approached about it, she was ecstatic."

Dawn had never dealt with a million dollar deal, let alone a $27 million deal. She immediately went to work, applying what she had learned in graduate school – "To be big, you have to think big." She boasted about their firm, said that they were global traders of every commodity. She even had a friend of Darrin's come in and pay her fifty dollars to record her voice. The woman had a British accent, and when people called TIGS, they heard her voice on the answering machine: "Welcome to Technology Integration Group Services, Inc. your worldwide supplier of IT products and services. Press 1 for sales, 2 for customer support, 3 for accounting, 4 for the company directory, and 0 for the operator."

One of the things that inspired her was her father's success and how far he had come from the days of living at the YMCA and eating chicken from a chicken shack's garbage. She figured that working with Emad on his telecom deal would bring in a good commission, expand her brother's company, and lead to what every small business and American family hopes for, which is to enjoy a better life. "Isn't that what capitalism is about?" she asked herself as she tried all she could to get vendors to give her a quote, but none would. Iraq was like AIDS – no one wanted to touch it.

After many failed attempts, she and Emad decided to

drop the telecom project. Months later, Emad returned, this time wanting to work on a different telecom deal worth about $10 million. He requested used equipment which would be delivered to Turkey. He said that there was a partner involved, Dresser International, which somehow was tied to Dick Cheney's Halliburton.

"Dick Cheney?" Issa nearly gasped. "Weam, this case can have monumental implications. This could be the Roe vs. Wade that overturns the Patriot Act. The Patriot Act is in direct violation of the Constitution. The government has a constitution to uphold the Constitution. You've got a great story here, and not one you'll find outside on the streets like you would a dead squirrel! I can approach Vincent Bugliosi and Richard Fine to help out with the case. Now, I can't guarantee they will get involved, but I definitely can talk to them about it."

A strong odor filled the house, and I realized I had left the vegetables boiling too long, but I did not care. I suddenly felt energized about my work, not tired and fearful. I imagined Dawn and Linda reuniting and the Hanna family being happy once again.

"I mean, Darrin and Dawn were pillars of this community," he said. "Darrin was not some guy building Nintendo games. He was finding safe areas during hurricanes to save peoples' lives! Dawn got a full college scholarship in the honors program and she studied abroad! Her father was no ordinary immigrant. He risked his life for the United States Government."

I was so exhilarated, I couldn't wait to wash the food and spices off of my hands and begin writing this story.

"What the government did is coercion," he said. "They manipulated the situation. This is entrapment! This CIA guy comes along with a huge money-making deal and Dawn is, of course, elated! The law was made to protect American citizens, not the opposite. What the prosecutor and judge did is abuse their position in office. It is malice. It is what King George used to do. With no recourse, King George threw people in jail as a matter of national security."

My writing wings expanded wider and wider, reaching from one end of the house to the other.

"One thing I do recommend, Weam," he said, abruptly switching to a suspenseful voice. The way he talked reminded me of Alfred Hitchcock with an Arabian/Californian accent. "First talk to your husband about this project, about the risks involved."

My heart dropped. "What risks?"

"I don't know. You might encounter some problems from the government."

"Like how?"

"Like, say for instance, you might suddenly get audited. Or maybe something else."

There was dead silence.

"Do you have anything to worry about?"

"I don't think so," I said, barely able to speak.

My phone's call-waiting clicked.

"Issa, that's Linda on the other line. Can I call you at another time?"

"Sure, sure! No worries!"

"Hi, Linda."

"Hey Weam. Did you get a chance to talk to Emad?"

"Yes."

"Well, what did he say?"

"He's up for the interview."

"Oh great! What a relief. Can't wait to tell Dawn. Weam, thanks so much. You're an angel. You really are."

"Thanks," I said thinly, feeling as if I was walking into a cauldron of sizzling soup.

Since September 11, 2001, Arab, Muslim, and Middle Eastern immigrants, including my family, encountered escalating discrimination at the hands of the US government and private citizens. If the Department of Homeland Security identified an individual as a potential terrorist, then he was subject to state monitoring, detention, deportation, special reporting requirements, and "voluntary" interviews. Did I really want to deal with all that?

CHAPTER 9
Is it a Story or is it Espionage?

"Unfortunately, I will not be able to interview Mr. Emad for the documentary because the issue is sensitive and not appropriate for my network and other TV satellites."

I read the email from Gina, a broadcaster who worked in London for a major Arabic television station. I emailed her back. "Is there someone else in London that you could recommend to interview him?"

"Sorry, I don't have any other recommendations."

"Thanks for your efforts," I wrote.

For safety purposes, Emad no longer lived in England but somewhere else in Europe. He was, however, getting an eye surgery in London during the first week of October. He would remain in the city for a few days to recover and then return home. I had to find a film crew to interview him as quickly as possible, before he left the country. Otherwise, the documentary would be missing the most important component of the story – him.

As I scrolled over my list of contacts, I couldn't stop thinking about Gina's response. It made me feel uneasy. This woman had happily agreed to interview Emad until she found out he was once a CIA operative. She didn't live in the United States, her face was not going to be shown on camera, and she was afraid to *interview*, simply *interview*, him. I tried to reason the situation in my head. Maybe the big TV stations she worked for were funded by the US government or terrorist groups. I called a local videographer of Iraqi origin and told him the situation.

"You've got to be kidding me," he said. "People don't want to interview this guy? Well, I have plenty of friends in the UK who work independently and would take this project in a heartbeat. What time is it right now? One o'clock. I should be able to get a hold of them in the next couple of hours and get back to you."

Relieved, I made a cup of coffee and cuddled beside my children. We watched *Max and Ruby* as the sunlight extended its arms through our windows, like a colorful quilt, its reflection covering the majority of the earth inside my home. The videographer called back and said, embarrassed, "These guys…They're too afraid to get involved. Can you believe it?"

"Afraid of what?"

"I don't know – just afraid. The US Government is involved here, you know."

"No, I do not know," I said. "I thought we're allowed to do legal things here."

"All over the world, there's a lot of political tension for Arabs, especially Iraqis. But if I was there, I wouldn't be afraid to interview him."

After we hung up, I called Issa and told him what had happened. We rationalized the filmmakers' reasons for not wanting to interview the CIA operative. Perhaps they were not citizens of the United Kingdom, and given the Islamophobia and Arabophobia going around the western world after 9/11, they probably feared that any involvement in government matters would cause their deportation or place them on the No-Fly list.

"I have a question," he said. "How do we really know that this guy is a CIA operative?"

"Well, the government never denied it." I put my coffee on the table. "Hold on a minute. Let me read you something." I crawled away from my children's clutches and went to my desk. I shuffled through the stacks of paper to find the documents where, a few weeks before Dawn reported to prison, the district court denied the motion for a new trial. "Here's one reason why the government claims they did not reveal to the jury the CIA agents' involvement." I read from one of the documents. "They say, 'Because it would have confused and inflamed the jury and taken their focus away from the elements of the charged offenses.'"

"It says that?"

"Yes."

"I am shocked that they have the audacity to say this – on paper! Was there anything in the trial to hint that Emad was a CIA operative?"

"Yes, let me find it here."

The transcripts were stacked on my desk in order of dates. On September 10, 2008, the first witness in the Hanna trial took the stand, Dean. Dean worked in sales at a recycling telecom company in the UK. He signed an immunity agreement so that the government would not be able to prosecute him for his involvement in the deal even though he claimed he was not at all suspicious about the fact that the destination of the equipment his company sold to Emad and Dawn was going to Turkey. Dean described how, when Emad visited him at work, he talked about the system's configuration, said that it would be set up like a pipe, a mobile network connecting two points and serving 100,000 subscribers. Dean thought this wasn't a typical configuration for this network. Since most of the customers would be walking around town, it was more common to build a network starting in a city and then expanding it outwards.

Emad explained to Dean, "The traffic will be very bursty, so at times there would be virtually nobody using it and then at other times everybody would be on the phone all at once. It's basically for use in emergency situations."

"What do you mean, like an earthquake?" Dean asked.

Emad nodded. "Or war."

After Dean gave his testimony, Prosecutor Michael Martin asked him, "Did Emad say anything to you about the US government?"

"He did," Dean said. "He said the project for the new network in Turkey is backed by the US government, but that they couldn't be seen to be involved in it. So they were working through his company, ATS (Advanced Technical Systems)."

"The US government was working through Emad and ATS, that's what he said?"

"That's what he said, yes."

"Did he ask you to keep this quiet?"

"He did. He asked me not to mention it to anybody."

"During any time when you were in contact with Defendant Dawn Hanna, Defendant Darrin Hanna, or with Emad, did you ever see any indication that the US government was involved?" the prosecutor asked.

"No."

"This is unbelievable!" Issa said.

"What if I go to London to interview Emad?" I asked.

"Don't even think about it. This has the CIA's name on it, so you might not come back."

What was wrong with everyone? Were they watching too many James Bond movies, or were their fears legitimate? Their fears could not be legitimate, I thought, because they reminded me of my childhood days in Iraq when, in our sturdy, thick-brick built home, my family was too scared to say Saddam's name, even if it was the middle of the night and the entire country was sound asleep. I'd often wondered, were there ghosts in the room spying on us? And if so, what would happen if these ghosts told Saddam that we'd mentioned his name?

When we received letters or gifts in Iraq from my oldest brother in America, everyone's faces glowed with restrained delight to hide their happiness so the neighborhood would not notice. They didn't want Saddam to know we had a brother in America. That might then spoil our attempt to flee his Baathist regime. I had never met this Saddam, but the mention of his name brought along terror.

One night I remember my oldest sister and a few relatives gathering around for a late tea. They chatted about ghosts, neglecting to notice the children sitting around them on the floor. I was scared by what I had heard, and the next morning I woke up to a man's face a centimeter or two away from my face. He was as white as snow and as flat as a cardboard. He slowly flowed over me from my chin and up to my forehead, like an open palm passing over a dead person's face to close their eyes. He was not ugly and actually had handsome features, but there was a seriousness and darkness about him that frightened me to where I could not move or scream.

Later, after I got dressed for school, I stepped into the backyard and saw that same face, this time floating in midair like a balloon. Its aura staring at me, it inhaled the energy around me as if smoking a cigarette. Its lungs had the capacity to feast on the ashes and filter without moving or frying its lips. The face appeared again on my walk to school. It made a few more visits before it stopped haunting me. About five years later, it returned when I was living in America. This time I did scream. I screamed so loud that I woke up the entire house. Everyone rushed to see if I was okay. When they learned it was only a nightmare, they went back to sleep. Almost thirty years later, at a writer's retreat, a woman who loved and sought ghosts started a storytelling circle. As I listened to everyone's ghost tales, I said, "That was Saddam's face! I was just too young and afraid to identify it."

I was shocked at my own discovery, and today I wonder what all that fear was about. Did Saddam and his intelligence service really not know about our American relatives and attempts to go to the United States? The 1968 change in US migration law allowed for a large number of immigrants from Iraq, and the migration of Chaldeans increased substantially. That same year was when Saddam helped carry out a bloodless coup, led by Ahmad Hassan Al Baker, who became president of Iraq after the coupe. Saddam Hussein became vice president.

The stream of Chaldean immigrants who came to the United States continued throughout the 70s and 80s – about 45,000 in 1986 and 75,000 by 1992 – until the start of the Gulf War, when the United States placed restrictions on immigration from Iraq. Unless they had someone serving in the military, Chaldean families were normally not stopped by the Iraqi government from coming to America. Rather, they were stopped by the immigration laws here in the United States. Or they were stopped by their own economic conditions. To immigrate to the United States, one had to have the money to do it, especially if they had a family to support, because they would have to live in Jordan, likely without jobs, for quite a while.

Saddam had mostly injected into his people a weapon commonly used in politics but rarely mentioned by anyone, and that is the mythology of the boogeyman. Asaad Kalasho, a well-known Iraqi American radio host and businessman once asked me, "Did Saddam ever hurt you or anyone in your family?"

"No," I answered.

"Did he ever hurt anyone you know?"

There was one man, artist and historian Amer Hanna Fatuhi. He refused to draw portraits of Saddam, refused to participate in an annual Baath Party Exhibit, and refused, as head of a visual arts magazine, to glorify the regime by writing articles about Saddam and his son, Oudai. He was interrogated on numerous occasions. He was never sentenced to jail, but he did endure torture from members of the regime and was sentenced to death three times. He fled Iraq as a result of political persecution.

I'd heard of another man, a communist whom I never met. His nephew told me that the government arrested him three times, each time warning him to stop practicing communism and anti-Saddam campaigns. He did not stop, despite his families' pleas. His wife and children begged him to put them ahead of his communist ideology, but he refused. The next time they arrested him, they sent him home in a casket. His nephew said to me, "He was warned repeatedly, but he cared more about the cause than anything else. I'll never forget the smile on his face when they arrested him."

Other stories I knew of had to do with men in prison for money laundering or export violations. No torture was involved, and their parents or wives quickly got them out of prison through bribes.

"Did you leave Iraq because of your fear of Saddam or to have your brothers avoid the army?" asked the radio host.

"Well, both..."

"What was the leading factor?"

"I think it was to avoid the war," I said. Then I asked him, as he was once friends with Dawn's uncle, Najib, "Was Najib really a spy?"

"Since 1991, anyone who was not anti-Saddam was considered 'a spy.' I was even at one point interrogated, but nothing came of it because they had no proof against me."

He then said, "Answer me this question. Since Saddam's fall, what parts of the world have become safer?"

Sandy, a British woman who worked for the United Nations, supervised the 2009 Iraqi independent elections in Michigan. We met at the place the independent elections were being held and made a connection when she and I expressed our views that the elections were in total disarray, so she gave me her business card. Sandy was later stationed in Afghanistan, and she knew a lot of reporters all around the world. When I told her I was looking for a filmmaker in London, fast, she introduced me to a British woman named Katia. Katia really cared about Dawn's plight, felt the subject was a humanitarian issue since someone was "languishing in prison." She wished me luck in what she called a "worthy cause," but the day she was scheduled to interview Emad, she called early in the morning, her voice filled with qualms.

"I'm sorry, Weam," Katia said. "I will not be able to interview Emad."

"Why? What happened?"

"I'm sorry. I really am. Close friends of mine strongly advised me against getting involved. They work for top publications and television stations in Washington and London."

I stepped outside so I would not wake up the kids. "I don't understand what the big deal is," I said. "We're just telling a story."

"This is espionage! It's plain espionage!"

I was not sure how this was espionage, but I did not argue. The tremble in her voice said that no way in hell would she sit across from someone associated, now or before, with the Central Intelligence Agency.

"I suggest that you, as a wife and a mum, take extra precaution or…" She hesitated. "Reconsider taking on this project. Honestly, it is not safe to do it, at least not independently. Perhaps if you worked under the umbrella of the BBC or Amnesty, you'd have protection."

I was no longer thinking about the project, but about Linda and Dawn. How would I break the news to them? Linda, Toby, and the film crew planned to meet at my home in a few hours. Maybe this was for the best, I consoled myself as I poured a fresh cup of coffee and sat in the chair outside. I didn't want to give Linda and Dawn false hopes and waste too much time and energy on this case. The 1991 Gulf War was an unjust war. The sanctions were an unjust law. The 2003 US-led invasion was a second unjust war. These crimes were not only left without a slap on the hand, but the government used them to prosecute, detain, and, in some cases, torture and deport people. On February 15, 2003, weeks before the 2003 invasion, more than ten million people from all over the world marched against the war, and yet the war took place as if none of the ten million people mattered.

Bugliosi, one of the greatest prosecutors in the twentieth century, along with a number of European countries, labored for years to bring charges against former President Bush, and even though evidence of Bush's crimes are as clear as a big fat fly in white milk, making opening a case against Bush as easy as opening the refrigerator door, no case has been opened. Two CIA operatives risked their lives to tell the truth about Dawn and they got nowhere. My niece said that Dawn's attorney was one of the best attorneys in Michigan and he couldn't get her acquitted. What could a documentary or a book do? Who was I to make a difference, through any form of media, especially remembering the lies Glaspie said to Saddam when they met on July 25, 1990, the day that she gave him the green light to enter Kuwait.

Saddam had complained about the continuous and persistent US media campaign against him, said it was full of untrue stories. Glaspie responded, "I saw the Diane Sawyer program on ABC, and what happened in that program was cheap and unjust. And this is a real picture of what happens in the American media, even to the American politicians themselves. These are the methods the western media employs. I am pleased that you add your voice to the diplomats who stand up to the media. Because your appearance in the media, even for five minutes, would help us to make the American people understand Iraq. This would increase mutual understanding. If the American president had control over the media, his job would be much easier."

If? I thought.

Wearing her cotton night robe, the neighbor across the street came out into her open, spotless, tidy, blue-painted garage. She lit a cigarette and started talking on the phone. She did that several times a day, her conversations mostly "he said, she said" – or at least those were the ones I overheard. The rest of the street was still quiet. After a while, I went back inside and decided that Katia's call was a sign not to get involved in Dawn's case. I did not want to jeopardize my welfare and that of my family's.

The organ started playing. I had been living in the same

house for over five years and still I did not know from which neighbor's house the organ sound came from and how it was so loud. Every now and then, sometimes daily, I heard it early in the morning. It was not the worst organ playing, but the music was dark and lasted for about fifteen minutes.

I made a pot of coffee. Soon my children woke up and the film crew arrived. They sat around the kitchen table discussing how we were going to shoot the documentary, even after I told them we might never start shooting. I tried to graciously kick them out, but as they ignored me, I saw, through the glass door, Toby and Linda approaching the house. Toby held a large tray of baklava and Linda was dressed in a floral dress. She looked like she was attending a baptism. The view of the suburban homes behind them and the green grass beneath their feet made for a perfect happy picture of a man and his wife going to visit their grandchildren.

In his mid-sixties, Toby looked younger despite his silver white hair. He resembled his brothers, Najib and Raad, in looks, but not in personality or lifestyle. Toby had once worked for the National Museum of Iraq. There, he mostly dealt with foreigners who influenced his desire to better himself elsewhere, in a country that offered freedom and opportunities. He moved to the United States.

When I first met him a few days prior, I learned that Toby had an impressive list of accomplishments. In the court transcripts, he was regularly referred to as a store owner even though, for years, he had worked as an advisor and translator for a US contractor in Iraq and had security clearance to work with multiple branches of the US government. He saved a number of lives in the war. Before that, for nine years in Sterling Heights, he was a chairperson on the advisory board. He had once been a member of the Chaldean Federation of America and got an award plaque as a result of his contributions to the community. For twelve years, he was a liaison in the Seven Mile area of Detroit. He helped clean up crime by working hand-in-hand with the police. He explained to the police the backgrounds of the Chaldean elderly men who hung out at coffee shops so that they wouldn't continue to raid the coffee shops with cultural illiteracy. One time a policeman shot a child and the people, outraged, were determined to burn the precinct. Toby negotiated and talked to the people, went door to door to calm everyone down.

I poured coffee for Linda and Toby and brought the cups to the table. "Katia called today. She says she can't do the interview."

Linda's tears started gushing, and I went looking for a box of Kleenex with my daughter pulling on my shirt and asking for apple juice. I told my daughter to hold on, and then the phone rang. It was Dawn's attorney, Deday LaRene. He informed me that for ethical purposes, especially since Dawn's case was under appeal, he would have to decline being interviewed. He felt that it would not serve Dawn's interests and may even harm her.

"Uh-huh," I said. I totally forgot that I had called him the day before. I had asked him for an interview, to which he'd basically replied, "The media is a bunch of hogwash!" Those were not his exact words, but they carried that exact tune. To be polite, he had promised he would think it over and call me back.

"Mr. LaRene, forget about the interview. I need your help

here," I said, observing the chaos in my home. In one corner, Linda was crying over the production producer's shoulder. In another corner, the film crew passionately discussed the scene shots that may never take place. Glued to me and staring at all of the excitement were my children.

"Sure," he said.

I updated him about what had happened, told him about how a number of film crews had dropped out of this project because of the subject matter, the most recent one defining it as "espionage." I told him about prominent members of the community advising me not to get involved, one of them even saying, "Those people [the government] are big guns. You don't want to mess around with them." Words you would expect to hear while watching *The Godfather Saga*.

"As a mother, I'm afraid to take on this project," I said. "I don't know if it's safe, but I'm also afraid of backing out and hurting the Hanna family any more than they've already been hurt."

"I don't see how a documentary could, in and of itself, hurt anyone," he said. "As for the filmmakers, I don't see why they are scared. What Emad is saying is hearsay. You are just documenting what *he* is saying. Furthermore, what he has said is already in the public domain, so you are not bringing anything new into light."

Yes, that was exactly how I saw it, but why didn't the others see it the same way? I was no more a lawyer than they were. I probably wasn't much smarter either. I may even be a big fool for being the only one who couldn't detect the dangers that others were able to detect. Maybe my husband, children, and housework had weakened parts of my sanity.

I hoped that Dawn's family would simply forget about the whole thing and make it easier for me to follow other peoples' abandonment.

I thanked LaRene for his help and we hung up. Toby then pointed at his cell phone and asked me if I could speak to Darrin.

"My dad told me what happened," he said. "If it's possible, we want you to go ahead with the documentary."

"How?"

"You can interview Emad through Skype, can't you?"

"That's not the point. The other day you said some people in Washington warned you that getting media attention might work against Dawn."

"Yes. We were told that politicians didn't like publicity that showed them in a negative light. That they might get so annoyed with us, they would deny Dawn the appeal."

"Well, doesn't that worry you?"

"No! No matter what they say, we'll never give up. We won't give up, ever. I don't care if nobody will face this case and say this is wrong! And if the appeal fails…I mean, I hope the appeal succeeds, although I have little faith from what I've seen in our justice system. It doesn't seem to work very well."

We were quiet momentarily.

"What I'm concerned about is my mom," he said. "Can you make sure that she in no way gets involved in any of this?"

"Darrin, it's because of your mom that I am involved."

"But these ups and downs, this excitement, could severely hurt her. She could be doing other, more productive things with her life."

"Like what?"

He didn't understand. He was not a parent yet.

"Darrin, I'm getting another call. Can we talk later?"

I clicked over.

"Hi, *habbibti* Weam, how are you? This is Nidhal!"

Oh Christ! I thought. I loved this woman, but it would be hard for me to listen to a this conversation with so many people and emotions dispersed in my house.

"Did you get my email for the fundraiser party coming up October 22?" she asked. "Tickets are only $40 and this includes dinner and appetizers. I am going to Iraq this winter with a medical and surgical container that is worth $650,000, so your support means a lot."

Nidhal, an attractive green-eyed pharmacist, was considered a saint by many Iraqis in Iraq. She began her humanitarian work in 2003 after she had viewed the Iraqis' suffering on television, and in 2007, she founded For Victims of War and Poverty, today called One World Medical Mission.

As she recounted the horrific conditions of the hospitals and patients in Iraq, I recalled the children's hospital and the Amiriyah shelter that had touched my heart so deeply, they were the only two places I wanted to visit when I was in Iraq.

CHAPTER 10
Unusual Places to Visit in Baghdad

Two of my cousins in Baghdad had vehicles and said they'd take me wherever I wanted to go. My itinerary list was not long. I told them I wanted to see two places: the children's hospital that treated those wounded in the war or hurt by the sanctions and the Amiriyah shelter that was bombed during the Gulf War.

"You want to see the Amiriyah shelter?" one cousin asked, surprised, possibly even concerned.

The Amiriyah shelter, built by a company from Finland and designed to withstand a nuclear bomb, was used in the Iran-Iraq War and the Persian Gulf War until February 13, 1991, when, at 4:30 am, while the majority were sleeping in bunkers stacked against the wall – it was said that some children were watching cartoons so they would not be frightened – two F-117 stealth fighter bombers each dropped on the shelter two-thousand-pound, laser-guided "smart bombs" that evidently were not too smart or well-guided, because they caused what is considered the single largest civilian massacre in modern air warfare.

The first "smart bomb" gave off a terrible high pitched whine as it cut through twelve feet of armored concrete, peeling away the protective cover. Neighborhood residents heard screams as people tried to get out of the shelter. Minutes later, the second bomb followed the path cut by the first bomb. The screaming instantly stopped as people staying in the upper level were burned by the temperature that rose to a thousand degrees centigrade (1832 Fahrenheit) while boiling water from the shelter's water tank and oxygen canisters killed those below.

Over 400 people were killed, mostly women and children because the men and older teenage boys had left the shelter to give women and children some privacy. Eight of those children belonged to Um Greyda, who then moved into a caravan beside the shelter, becoming a primary guide for visitors. Later, Um Greyda helped create a memorial inside the shelter that featured photographs of the victims and other photographs of their mutilated bodies, brown patches of dried blood and visible, blackened, smooth and pasty human skin that had melted into the walls and floors.

I also wanted to go to the hospitals where children were rushed to, their screams of pain heard all over the corridors, their liver and kidneys damaged due to over 300 tons of depleted uranium that was used during the war. Bishop Gumbleton of Detroit, one of the leading advocates for the lifting of the sanctions on Iraq, talked a great deal about these hospitals. Depleted uranium has metal poison and radiation. If a person breathes even one gram into their lungs, it is the same as getting an x-ray every hour for the rest of their shortened life. The uranium cannot be removed, there is no treatment, no cure, and it will poison Iraqi civilians and US servicemen for decades.

In these hospitals were the wounded and maimed due to bomb shrapnel; the extremely deformed newborns due to uranium; the infants who suffered from heavy diarrhea due to malnutrition because the air strikes destroyed much of the country's power supply, severely affecting the water and sanitation systems. Many mothers were unable to produce enough milk, and buying milk wasn't really an alternative, perhaps because the baby milk formula factory, the only source of infant formula food for children one year and younger in Iraq, was bombed a week into the raids, or with the dinar no longer having any value, they couldn't afford it.

Whatever the reasons, 5,000 children under the age of five started to die each month as a result of the war and sanctions. A special cemetery for children was built after the Gulf War to accommodate the situation.

"Why do you want to go see the children's hospital and the shelter?" my aunt asked. She gave her son Bashar a small handbag of garbage and told him to throw it outside. She then looked at me. "A girl like you shouldn't see such awful things, especially not the shelter. They've turned it into a memorial in remembrance of those who died." She looked at Bashar. "Why are you still standing there?"

He sprinted out of our sight.

"The victims' remains and possessions were left untouched," she said. "Some of the children's toys and their clothes are still lying on the floor beside a bunch of flowers brought there by mourners..." Her eyes moved away from me. "There are other things there that you just should not see."

She was talking about the bodies that were carbonized with the walls, floors, and ceiling. I was told that visitors of the shelter could easily recognize the shapes of the victims' faces and bodies, one of which was a mother holding her child. In one corner of the ceiling, there were handprints and actual hands, some belonging to children. When the shelter was bombed, the heat had fused its doors to the door frames. People and children, desperate to get out, climbed over each other's shoulders and tore at the ceiling's concrete with their hands. When the bodies were pulled out of the building, many of the hands remained stuck to the ceiling.

My aunt asked, "And besides, who do you think can take you there?"

"I can take her!" Bashar said.

His presence startled us as we had not realized he'd returned.

My aunt gave him a look like he would get it soon if he did not shut up. "No, you will not! A girl like her should not be subjected to this type of sorrow!"

"But I want to be subjected!"

"He couldn't take you even if he tried. He doesn't know where the shelter or the hospital is."

"Yes, I do," he said. "I've gone there before. I can take her. It's easy."

"Bashar, for heaven's sakes!" She rolled her eyes and placed her hands on her hips. She turned to me. "Trust me,

daughter, it's not as simple as you think. Going to these places is a big process."

I was determined to go, regardless of what she said.
However, because I didn't know the rules of the country, and
there were no tourist offices, and it wasn't very smart for a
woman to just get up and find her way around the city on her
own, I went to my other cousins and explained my predicament. They listened at first, and then they laughed hysterically when they heard that my aunt's son had offered to take me.

"Unless you're an Iraqi citizen, you need to apply to the
embassy first," they explained. "They'll evaluate your request,
maybe even question what business you have going there,
and three or four weeks later they will either grant or deny
you entrance, by which time you would have returned to
America."

"Why is this so complicated?" I asked, dumbfounded.

They said that, after the unexpected second US bombings in 1998, Saddam didn't allow anyone without authori-
zation to enter areas that dealt with or were affected by the
war. In the past he caught many spies lingering around there.
The second bombings they were talking about were Desert
Fox, which some people called a distraction from Clinton's
impeachment scandal. It was a major four-day bombing
campaign of key Iraqi military installations that President
Clinton ordered without UN Security Council approval and
it occurred at the same time the US House of Representatives was conducting the impeachment hearings. While the
bombing was ongoing, the Vanguards of Conquest, a branch
of the Egyptian Islamic jihad, issued a bulletin to Islamist
groups calling for attacks against the United States "for its

arrogance" in bombing Iraq.

With regards to the spies, my relatives were talking about when the CIA recruited officers within Saddam's inner circle to help in a military coup d'état in 1996. The plotters, which included Ahmad Chalabi and Ayad Allawi, two rivals who both tried to reign over Iraq after the fall of Saddam, were told that the US would recognize them as Iraq's new leaders. They were given discrete mobile phones with direct lines to the CIA, but a special unit of Iraqi intelligence was ahead of the game. They burst into homes across Baghdad and began arresting the operatives, at least 200 of them, eighty of whom were executed. Then Saddam's agents found the CIA's phones and an Iraqi intelligence officer placed a call. A US agent answered. He was reportedly told, "Your men are dead. Pack up and go home."

I contacted my chaperone Raad and asked if he could help. He said with a positive grin, "I can take you anywhere you want. I have connections." Then, along with his so-called connection, Raad drove me to one of the hospitals. I waited in the car and watched the men stand at the front entrance of the hospital with the director of the hospital. It didn't look good.

As he listened to the director, Raad put his hands on his hips, looked up to the sky, then down to the ground. He scraped the bottom of his shoe against the cement, looked up to the sky again, then slowly walked back to the car.

"This guy says our visit has to be authorized by the government because you're an American." He glanced back to where his connection was still talking to the director of the hospital. "I guess they don't trust Americans!" He roared with laughter, banged on top of the car, and said, "Let's go!"

CHAPTER 11
An Alternative to the Iraq War

Look at how many lives we lost in the invasion? We could have done it Emad's way and saved tens of thousands Iraqi and American lives, but instead, my mom lost her daughter and many moms lost their sons, the way the USA operates.

When I received this email from Dawn, I forwarded it to Emad and asked, "What did Dawn mean by that?" He wrote:

It's very simple. My idea was to hit Saddam only, to locate him and blast him away. But Bush and his cronies did not want a simple solution. They wanted an all-out war and to occupy Iraq, steal its wealth and keep it dependent on American goods for as long as possible.

I replied:

> I guess people are so advanced now that
> they've thrown simple ways of doing things
> out the door. Like the story of Jennifer
> Hawke-Petit. She and her two daughters, ages
> eleven and seventeen, were raped and burned
> to death as the police sat outside their house
> for over forty minutes "preparing" what to
> do. Yet two days after this horrendous crime,
> Dawn and Darrin received a way over-the-
> top arrest treatment for an export violation.

Dawn had just arrived back to the United States from a twenty-one-day trip to Trinidad, where she was finalizing the purchase of scrap metal and working on a housing project with a local development company. When she got to Miami International Airport in transit to Detroit, the only thing that struck her as odd was that when she went through US Customs, she simply went through for the first time in years. She didn't receive a secondary screening, the way she had in sixteen of her seventeen previous trips abroad. Dawn called her younger brother Darrin to tell him how surprised and relieved she was that finally, in the summer of 2007, being tormented by the US Government was coming to an end.

"Customs didn't harass me for once," she said.

Three days later, on July 25, she came to work a little after nine o'clock. At thirty-four years old, Dawn had a master's degree in international marketing and was vice president of sales at Technology Integration Group (TIGS), a small company in Rochester Darrin started when he was eighteen years old so that he and several of his friends would have summer jobs rather than work at McDonald's. Before Dawn joined in 1998 as an international broker, the company's principal focus was to sell computer hardware, software, and technology services. Another family member who worked at TIGS was Dawn's mother, Linda. She was the office manager. There were twelve employees that sat in a big open space area where the desks were pieced together like puzzles.

Dressed casually that day, having just returned from a trip and not in the mood to put on her usual attire, Dawn got herself a cup of coffee. On the way back to her desk, she noted that Darrin was with a few businessmen in the conference room, which had open windows that overlooked South Street, an industrial area of the small town of Rochester. She settled into her chair and turned on the computer. She had a lot of work to do and emails to sort out. She barely did any work, however, because just after 9:30 am, she heard a lot of stomping up the stairs.

Then Special Agent Brian Wallace and about eight others with bulletproof vests, each one armed with guns of all shapes and sizes, shoved their way into the office.

"No one move!" Wallace said. Holding up his badge, he flashed some paperwork in Dawn's face and handed the paperwork to her. "Dawn Hanna, arrest warrant! Export violation!"

Wallace was an investigative agent who worked for Immigration and Customs Enforcement. Dawn first met him four years prior when, in June of 2003, he and his men had similarly barged into the TIGS office with a search warrant. After receiving an anonymous phone call that Dawn Hanna and TIGS were involved in exported shipments for Global Systems for Mobiles (GSM) to Iraq, the Bureau of Homeland Security in 2003 began what was to become an exhaustive four-and-a-half-year investigation into the Hanna family and TIGS.

Agent Brian Wallace first used a technique referred to as "trash pull," where he contacted the garbage collectors and told them he wanted to go through the trash that TIGS threw out. In the summer of 2003, he claimed to have gone through the garbage about eight to ten times and ended up finding a document, which later became known as the "Dear Charles" letter. He took the document to the magistrate to obtain a search warrant for TIGS.

Dawn and her family questioned the trash pull technique, as they were never shown pictures of this letter with the proper tagging and labeling of evidence. They were informed of the exact day the trash was pulled, and when Dawn researched it, it turned out to be a Friday. However, garbage day was Monday. The Hannas had a clear recollection of that because, after the weekend, they had smelly garbage from Friday's lunches. It was a chore deciding who was going to take the trash bags to the curb. Sometimes Linda and her husband Rick cleaned the office on Sunday to prepare for the work week, but they never put it out on Friday, as it could not sit all weekend.

Once the search warrant was granted, on June 25, 2004, Wallace and about eight of his men barged into TIGS wearing bulletproof vests and holding weapons. Everyone in the office was ordered to go into the conference room, and if anyone wanted to use the bathroom, they had to be escorted there by a guard. That day, Dawn had come into work later, so she didn't witness the initial drama. Darrin was away on a business trip. Linda called him to tell him what was happening, and he said, "Well, give them what they want and call me if you need anything."

After all the employees were secured in one location to make sure they step away from their work areas so no one would touch any of the documents or computers, computer forensics agents began to work on the email server as quickly as possible. Wallace had one of the agents from another office come with a mobile van where the agent could copy hard drives on-site as opposed to taking the hard drives or the whole computer out and seizing them. Later, trained computer forensics agents extracted the raw data and put it in a format that was readable.

Wallace and his team walked out of TIGS that day with a load of files, leaving the Hannas wondering why the government would use such theatrics. It looked as if a SWAT team had come to raid a place in the Middle East. And why were they being blamed for Emad's deal?

At that point, this is what the Hanna family knew about Emad: He was born in Iraq as a Sunni Muslim of Kurdish origin. When he was a teenager, he moved to the United Kingdom with his family, where he attained British citizenship and ended up marrying a British woman. Linda met Emad when he came to Michigan to work with Dawn. One day Dawn had another obligation, so Linda picked up Emad from his hotel and brought him over for dinner. He sat on their couch and ate a humble meal, goulash, and played with her two dogs, Lucy and Katie, reddish, long haired, mini dachshunds.

To Linda, Emad seemed to be a regular person, a sincere businessman with a British accent. Emad had no children, but he did have a cat, a stray brown and black cat he'd picked up while living at his penthouse in Amman, Jordan. The cat's name was Nahla, and Nahla was very spoiled. She had a free run of the house and was friends with other strays and pets in the building complex. Emad's wife fed the other strays and pets as well. Nahla had two bowls of food set up for her in the kitchen. Emad really liked his cat and spoke of her with a smile. Before Dawn met the cat in person, she thought Nahla was Emad's daughter because of the way he spoke about her over the phone to his wife.

Whenever Dawn discussed with Emad the government's investigation into the telecommunications deal, he repeatedly assured her not to worry, that all would turn out okay. He told her that Agent Wallace had called him and, based on the information he'd provided Wallace, the matter was cleared up.

"Now they will leave you two alone," Emad had said to Dawn.

The United Kingdom jointly investigated this case until 2006, when they closed the investigation without any charges. Not in the United States. Every few months, they were contacted by Brian Wallace for the grand jury or someone was telling Dawn or Darrin that they were subpoenaed. The Hanna family felt that they were being stalked by a beast.

An officer told Dawn that she was under arrest for conspiring to knowingly and willfully export property from the US to Iraq in violation of the US embargo. He read her rights and immediately put her in handcuffs as another group of people headed for Darrin in the conference room. Shaking, Linda called Darrin. "Customs are here to arrest you and Dawn," she said.

In no time, Darrin came out of the conference room. He stood in the stairwell, where he was made to empty his pockets, then handcuffed. Dawn saw he was scared.

"Call the attorneys," Darrin told his mother.

A friend and work associate helped Dawn take off her necklace and cross. Dawn removed her rings and her watch and took her license out of her purse. She then wrote on a note, "Call the lawyer," with the lawyer's number and passed the note to her mother. Linda stood there in shock. At one point she started to cry.

"Don't worry, don't worry," Dawn said to her, even though she herself felt numb. But since she'd worked in the legal system before, she knew that she and her brother would be booked in and probably released on some bond.

As soon as her son and daughter were taken out of the office, Linda tried to compose herself enough to call the attorneys. The attorneys told her, "It's okay. Calm down. We will get Dawn and Darrin out."

But she remained frantic and rushed to the computer. She sent an email to Toby, who was working in Iraq. The email read, "They took Dawn and Darrin away." She knew that Toby would not get the email until he was in a safe location with computer access. She waited for him to call back later that day so she could tell him what had happened, which she described to everyone as a scene out of a gangster movie.

TIGS was located on 360 South Street, an industrial area of town commonly referred to as "under the bridge," referring to the bridge that brings one from the main road into the little quaint town of Rochester. It sort of separates the small industrial area from the commercial downtown boutiques, shops, and restaurants. Outside Dawn noticed people peeking through their windows and a few people on the street gawking. To her, Wallace seemed happy as he and his men quickly put Darrin into an SUV and her into another one. He had a smug look on his face.

She sat in the back while an Asian agent drove in the front with Wallace in the passenger seat. The first thing Wallace did in the car was call Barbara McQuade, the prosecutor, and tell her, "We have the Hannas."

"Okay, well, good, good," Dawn heard the response through the speaker. "Bring them downtown. I'll see you soon."

They cracked some sort of joke, Wallace laughed, and then he hung up.

In the other SUV, Darrin sat in the backseat, thinking, "They've got the wrong people."

The Hannas arrived to the Federal building after what felt like forever. In the parking area, Dawn and Darrin were told to stay away from each other, not to get too close. Inside, they were fingerprinted and put in separate cells. A woman came in to pat Dawn down. Dawn felt overwhelmed as she laid down on the bench and put her feet up. She was embarrassed and humiliated to be taken out in handcuffs in front of employees and friends she had worked with for over ten years. The government didn't have to do that, she thought. They didn't have to come in like SWAT and act like they were catching Bin Laden red-handed.

Both Dawn's lawyer and Darrin's lawyer were not happy about the spectacle that went on at TIGS's office. They felt that the government did not have to sensationalize the case by barging into the office, arresting Dawn and Darrin, and making a show. Instead they could have informed the attorneys of what was going on and had the Hannas voluntarily turn themselves in.

Darrin didn't care about that. When he met with his attorney, all he wanted to know was, "Can't we meet up with them and figure out what they're upset or confused about?"

"You know, that's not the way that this works," his attorney said. "At this stage of the game, things are past that."

Darrin sensed that what his nice-looking blond lawyer was politely telling him was, "This is not about them getting the wrong guys and trying to work this out. This is about winning against you, and they're against you now."

Later in the day, when they went before the magistrate, Dawn and Darrin entered a plea of not guilty and they got a $10,000 signature bond, so no money was involved. Darrin's attorney asked the magistrate if Darrin could attend a wedding in the Czech Republic coming up since he already had travel arrangements, and she said, "No."

They received a copy of the indictment and left the court.

"Go home and I will get with you in a few days," Dawn's

attorney said to her. "And get ready for the fight of your life."

At home, Dawn and Darrin learned that the government attorneys had labeled their case a terrorism case and that the media had followed without question. In a press release dated July 25, 2007, United States Attorney Murphy said, "Evading the US embargo on a hostile regime like Saddam Hussein's is a serious crime with punishing consequences that cannot be ignored. I applaud the excellent work by IRS, ICE, and the FBI in investigating this crime."

The media had a field day with the Hanna story, showing pictures of Saddam Hussein next to photos of both Dawn and Darrin along with military weapons and other war shots.

Quickly, the Hannas were branded "terrorists."

Emad was stunned by the outcome, but he still believed that the government would not take this as far as Dawn and Darrin feared it would go, to trial. Because, as he'd told Dawn on several occasions, "This will open a huge can of worms that the USA government does not want to open."

CHAPTER 12
Dawn Meets a Cool Man

It was early 2002. Emad and Dawn had not yet met in person but had exchanged a lot of emails where they had formed a love-hate business relationship. They didn't trust each other. She had told him TIGS was a multi-national firm and that she had traveled the world doing large-scale projects and he was small potatoes to her – a sales tactic to force him to buy the equipment he wanted that TIGS did not have. For her, this was Brokering 101 for Monkeys.

They decided to meet in person and discuss the telecom and other deals. "Let's have lunch in London," Emad said.

"How will I know what you look like?" Dawn asked Emad.

"I'll have a red carnation in my jacket. Just look for the good-looking man in the café."

They met at an informal coffee and sandwich shop located on Knightsbridge Road, home of many expensive shops like Harrods. It was crowded and crammed, like most London cafés.

Outside was cold and gray, the typical London weather in winter. Nearly sixty years old, Emad was short and stocky and hunched himself a bit when he walked. He wore a black pea coat and what Dawn described as transition glasses from the 1980s.

They sat down at a table, and Emad slowly examined the menu. Dawn was impressed by his outer appearance. She thought that he carried himself well and looked cool, although he did remind her of a cartoon character whom she could not pin point. Emad ordered iced tea. Lifting his head up, he looked at the menu from under the lower rims of his glasses. He slowly closed the menu and slowly said, "I'll have the Caesar salad. What do you fancy?"

"I'll have the same," she said. She did not really want to eat a Caesar salad, but she was a little nervous. Something about him made her nervous. He moved with precision and kept looking around the café, taking in the crowd, atmosphere, and his surroundings.

Not long afterward, he began to make her feel comfortable with his sense of humor and his knowledge of her father's Chaldean heritage and the business and political mindset of America. She was in awe. Thinking he was Jordanian, given that he also lived in Jordan, she had no idea how he knew so much. The two brainstormed about business they could do together both in the Middle Eastern and European markets. Emad asked her if she could get a Caterpillar forklift for a project he was working on.

"Of course, we can sell you anything," she said, thinking

that even if this millionaire businessman asked for pig shit she would find a way to deliver. "I have access to the company who is a direct agent for Caterpillar in the US."

At home, she went straight to the internet and yellow pages, calling some friends of hers in the construction industry, telling them she had a buyer for a forklift but no one to supply.

When Dawn first arrived in London, she stayed at the Holiday Inn in Earl's Court, a short walk to South Kensington and Notting Hill. Notting Hill Gate had many holistic little boutique shops, yoga studios, Pilates, and herbal spas. The upscale shops were in Knightsbridge. South Kensington was like the middle of the road. When she wanted to feel like she was in the city of Dearborn (nicknamed Arabic town in Michigan), she went to a place called Edgeware Road, where there were different Middle Eastern cultures and kabob shops, phone card centers, and internet cafés.

Dawn loved staying in London. She easily jumped into that lifestyle, felt a connection and belonging to the city more than she had felt in New York, Chicago, Rochester, or anywhere else. She even entertained the idea of settling there. She spent her mornings in the Covent Garden area, where there was an art fair, farmer's market, open theatre, festival-like atmosphere, café's, and many flea market-style stands that reminded her of Chinatown in New York – except that London was like a smaller, cleaner, and more posh area of New York.

She visited churches, castles, and monuments in England. The country's history and culture was amazing in comparison to what existed in the United States. She liked the ethnicity and people too, finding them very friendly and not judgmental. They did not tend to stare at her. On the weekends she tagged along with friends who partied first class, and she slept a lot because working with Emad was so fast paced that she hardly had any rest during the week. He shot questions at her constantly and wanted details upon details. He questioned every step she made, and she had to go over and over the same information quite often. He kept his eyes on new businesses popping up and was always available to come over for whatever required his attention or approval.

The Holiday Inn Dawn stayed at was an older hotel, but it was pretty Americanized with the exception of the staff, who were not all British although they had the British accent. The manager, Christian, was from the British West Indies. He was dark black with a British and Caribbean accent. Christian liked to peg people upon arrival by taking one look at them and noting where they were from. He couldn't guess that Dawn was American because her dark features threw him off. When he found out, he laughed and cheerfully said, "Yes, you are from de States, de United States."

Christian felt bad about often seeing Dawn arrive at the hotel late at night and sometimes miss breakfast. She didn't mind it so much, since she didn't like the English tea they served. One day he laughed at her after seeing she had gone grocery shopping at Sainsbury.

"How do you plan to prepare the food in your room?" he asked.

"Isn't there a microwave?"

"Yes, but it's on another floor and not that convenient to

get to."

She was at a loss for words. Seeing how she ran around like a loose chicken, he one day caught her in the lobby and gave her a key. "Go to the kitchen and see Robert," he said. "He will give you what you want."

Dawn started going into the kitchen and dining room to make her own breakfast of toast and an egg with coffee or just to get fruit and juices when the kitchen was closed. She felt like a stray cat, especially after being there for weeks at a time and constantly working around the clock with all the time zone differences. During her breaks, she bugged Christian at the concierge station and talked to him about culture, travel, economics, finance, and business since he was smart and had a great personality. The two laughed together when Americans and Canadians came in with too much luggage, then complained about the size of the elevator, or what Christian called "the lift," or when they complained about the English breakfast, which they weren't used to.

"America is such a vast country," Christian said to her. "Big, big, big everything. Big people. Big suitcases. Big coffee cups. Big gallons of milk. Big egos. Big wallet. Big mouth. Big government doing big, big things when they want something. But small mind, small mentality with an odd way of thinking and not very direct. Like they skate around things and offer a lot of innuendo."

The only thing she did not like about London was how expensive it could be. Even when business was doing well, she could shovel out so much money in the course of a day that sometimes she felt like a poor peasant living day by day. By the time she bought a phone credit, breakfast, or hit

Starbucks, took a few cab rides, ate lunch or popped into a shop for something, she easily burned through sixty pounds, roughly a hundred dollars, per day.

During each visit to London, Dawn stayed no less than a week, sometimes as long as three weeks. She met with Emad regularly. By now, he had left a strong impression on her. She began to look up to him. He was like a British accented history, a political and religious book packed into one. A Sunni Muslim, Emad could quote scripture from the Bible and the Torah. His wife was a British woman from Bristol whom he met when he first arrived to the UK at the age of sixteen. Yes, only one wife. He did not believe in the four wives theory and a lot of Islamic rules which he and Dawn laughed off because the rules did not make logical sense.

People of different backgrounds and religions naturally intrigued Dawn, but there was an extra intrigue that went with Emad. He wasn't the practicing type of Muslim, so to speak, or at least not a strict one like, say, the man from Turkey whom she dealt with. The Turkish man was so religious that he was up at the crack of dawn for the call to prayer and had to excuse himself during a meeting to go and pray. While Emad was quick to tell someone he was Muslim and he did believe in God and did pray, he did not openly practice his religion. Dawn never saw him go into a mosque. He ate pork. He had bacon and eggs for breakfast and, at other times of the day, didn't mind ordering a bacon cheeseburger and pizza with pepperoni. When she asked him, "You eat pork?" He responded, "Why not? It's tasty."

He even drank wine and beer, always raising his glass beforehand to say, "Cheers!"

Dawn liked hanging out with Emad and watching the way in which he operated with a moderate temperament. He was very relaxed and calculating, except when things got heated with the vendors. He would get a little angry if they didn't meet deadlines or suddenly changed prices on him. She noticed that he assessed a situation carefully and asked many questions. He spoke slowly and when someone, including herself, asked him a question, his first response was never to answer. He'd pause, then he'd look at the person with a puzzled look, and finally he'd say, "Okay, can you clarify?" Sometimes he answered a question with a question. Dawn was interested in his conversations because he was logical, often saying things like, "Well, logically..." or "Well, technically..." Then he would explain in detail what was on his mind.

One day, Emad visited Dawn unannounced at the Holiday Inn. It was around noon. He called her from the front desk.

"Hi, Emad. What's going on?"

"Nothing. Just popping in to see how you are coming along with things."

She came out to the business area to greet him. They sat together a bit and talked about general things, like the gloomy weather in England, his position at Hewlett-Packard in Saudi Arabia, his travels and engineering background.

"You look hungry," he said. "Do you want lunch?"

"Okay."

"Shall we wander up the High Street and see what we are hungry for? What do you prefer?"

"There is an Indian takeaway place just up the street."

"All right. We should walk and have a look."

They went to the Indian place where Christian had directed her to eat at early on. Emad took over fifteen minutes to examine the menu and in the end, they ordered a few dishes to share. They sat outside the café. Emad looked disappointed at the meal. She asked him what was wrong, and he said, "Well, nothing. But this is all fryer."

She had to stop and think until she figured out that he didn't like fried foods. "Kooh...all this fryer. It's not healthy."

"I love fried food," she said under her breath. "Can't get enough of it."

He toyed with his food and ate, slowly. "So Dawn, you are from the United States. What do you believe about 9/11?"

"I don't know," she said. "I used to think one way and then watching the media in Europe makes me wonder."

"It's hard to believe that someone was asleep at the wheel of counterintelligence and data was not reported, wouldn't you say? It was either that or else it was all part of a big plan for the United States to finally get into the Middle East for the natural resources at the expense of three thousand-plus people losing their lives."

Emad believed 9/11 was a conspiracy since Bush had many ties to Saudi Arabia and there was a rumor that many Jews didn't go to work that morning. Emad was not in the minority with his belief. The conspiracy idea was no big deal in the Arab world. Not even in Europe, where they'd already experienced similar conspiracies during Operation Gladio. Gladio was a far-right secret army under NATO auspices which carried out what they termed "false flag" operations, or terror attacks against innocent citizens in the 1960s, 1970s, and 1980s that were blamed on the radical left-wing groups in order to convince allied governments of the need for counter-action. Former Italian President Francesco Cossiga, who revealed the existence of Operation Gladio, publicly echoed Emad's words about the 9/11 conspiracy, adding that "this is common knowledge amongst global intelligence agencies."

The conspiracy idea should not have been a big deal in the United States either, given the revelations of Operation Northwood, a series of false-flag proposals that originated within the US government in 1962 but were rejected by the Kennedy administration. The proposals called for the CIA, or other operatives, to commit phony acts of terrorism like hijackings and bombings in US cities and elsewhere, then blame it on Cuba in order to create public support for a war against that nation, which had recently become communist under Fidel Castro.

After the first World Trade Center collapsed, one of our regular customers, a Native American who, in my books, I refer to as the Red Indian, came into the video store and pointed at the TV. There were images of people hanging on the steel bars. He said, "If the steel was so hot that it made the tallest buildings in the world collapse, how come it didn't burn these peoples' fingers and shoes?"

I remembered the Amiriyah shelter, where the 1832 Fahrenheit temperature melted 400 people as quickly as chocolate melts in a microwave. I had no answer for him. He left and returned to the video store later that same day. Grinning, he posed another question. "Did you hear about the third building that fell?"

"What third building?" I asked, handing a customer her change.

"The one that *poof*—" He illustrated the sound effect with his hands. "—magically fell on its own."

After living in the Holiday Inn, Dawn wanted to sample different areas of London, so she moved to the Hilton in Holland Park, a cute area about four blocks from Notting Hill Gate. Emad watched her for a while, saw her hotel hopping and moving around like a gypsy before he suggested they look for a flat in London to rent for a year and split the costs. That way he, too, would have a place, other than his in-laws', to stay and work while in London. By this time, Emad was spending his time between London and Jordan.

"I like living here, but I prefer the Middle East," he said. "London is good for business and all, but it's too open. You are on the front street and that's not suitable for families or any quiet lifestyle."

He ended up finding a two-bedroom, two-bathroom apartment at Hanger Lane Station in Ealing. The building had a gym, a private garage with two gates of security, and a butler. Mostly foreign people as well as diplomats lived there. Dawn, who liked working with Emad, found that he was also nice to live with. He knew his way around and where to find all the good deals.

When she stocked the cupboards with food from the local party store, he said, "Come on, Dawn. We need real food." He took her to IKEA and ASDA, a store similar to Walmart. At ASDA, he grabbed a giant cart and tracked down sales. They bought a TV, food, and house supplies, and as Emad loaded the car, he handed her the keys and said, "Now you will drive us home."

His gesture did not surprise Dawn. He often made casual decisions in order to teach her a thing or two.

"You need to migrate into the realistic way of living in a large city," he said, "rather than go broke taking cabs everywhere."

She almost killed him trying to maneuver through London's streets, so he suggested she take a driving class. Yet he was still brave enough to take her out late at night, on weekends, and even during traffic hours so she could learn to drive.

The flat was already furnished with a dirty eleven-piece pink sectional that Dawn said had to be changed. Emad told her she could furnish the place any which way she wanted, and she ended up buying leather couches and stone tables from an Italian furniture outlet in their area.

Emad liked working from the flat, where he had access to his tea and the TV. He typically watched BBC and other news channels all day long. She preferred a real office. They ended up sharing an office with colleagues whom Dawn did business with in the UK. That was more of Dawn's style, being able to ride the tube to work and hop over to Sloan Street or Harrods during her lunch hour.

Emad respected her space so that, even when they were at the flat at the same time, they lived somewhat separately. She was free to be herself, to be kind of a scattered mess and do ten thousand things at once as he calmly watched TV, made calls, and sipped tea. He did keep a pretty watchful eye on her, though, and tracked who was coming in and out. He did not encourage her to make friends other than the few business colleagues whom she had met and known before meeting him.

He had a few visitors on occasion, mostly family, it seemed. She wasn't sure, as she did not hang around when people came to see him. When his wife came on a few of the trips, she brought her stylish feminine touch with her. She grocery shopped and cooked for them.

Dawn found Emad's wife to be a delight. She had blonde hair and blue eyes and was petite, polite, and formal. The women took walks through Ealing together and had wonderful conversations. Like him, Emad's wife knew a lot about a lot of things. She informed Dawn of many shops to go to in London, and she even showed Dawn her purchases from Marks and Spencer, one of her favorite shops in Europe. She called it "Marks and Sparks."

Every time Dawn arrived in London after Emad was there or when he and his wife would come at the same time, he would have Chardonnay wine available and stocked in the fridge for them to drink. He didn't much care for white wine, but he made sure that whatever the women liked was always there. They would sit in the living room and watch television and get into really good conversations about current events and politics. Most of the time Dawn thought it was fun having Emad in London. Sometimes, though, it was a bit much because he was there all day, every day, and she would just need some space, but he never pushed himself on anyone and was kind of a quiet moving guy. He was good about being a ghost when necessary.

CHAPTER 13
The Real Intentions of the War

Emad was sixteen years old when he and his family went on vacation to England. Four days later, the 1958 revolution in Iraq happened. "It was the worst revolution we ever had," he said. "Had it not been for it, we would have been in our golden age, and the whole world would want to visit us."

There were many "golden ages" in Iraq. The country spans over 7,300 years and is home to some of the most important landmarks of the Judeo-Christian tradition, including the reputed Garden of Eden and Ur, the birthplace of patriarch Abraham. It is where writing, astronomy, and science were invented.

A more modern "golden age" of Iraq was when the Abbasid dynasty ruled most of the Muslim world from Baghdad, making the city the world's center of education and culture, where Christians and Muslims were said to have lived in peace and tolerance. Then the Mongol leader Hulagu

Khan came along in 1258 and set a match on the city, destroying the Grand Library of Baghdad, otherwise known as the House of Wisdom, along with thousands of irreplaceable historical, scientific, and artistic works. Iraq never regained its status as a center of culture and influence, but the words "golden age" continued to be attributed to different eras, one of which was during the Hashemite monarchy, which the British established.

Once Winston Churchill learned of Iraq's oil in the early 1900s, he vowed to liberate Iraq from its oppressive Turkish rule while countries like the United States and Germany complained to no avail that Britain was going into Iraq because of oil interests. After it liberated Iraq, Britain planted one Saudi king in Iraq and his brother in Jordan and with the help of France, sliced the Middle East like a cake, shared 95 percent of Iraq's petroleum between itself, France, and the United States, and then cut off Kuwait from the rest of Iraq. Before the 1920s, Kuwait was a district of Basra, Iraq's second largest city. Basra is part of the location of Sumer, the home of Sinbad the Sailor and a proposed location of the Garden of Eden.

For the thirty-eight years that the Hashemite royal family existed in Iraq, each king put forth a claim for Kuwait to be returned to Iraq. The British refused to consent until January 1958, when Iraq threatened that in July of that year, they would publish to the world secret documents they had between them. Britain finally consented and arranged for both parties to meet in London in July to sign the necessary papers. Prior to the meeting, on July 14, 1958, units of the Iraqi Army surrounded the royal palace, ordered the royal family and their servants to gather in the palace courtyard, told them to turn toward the wall, and gunned them down.

With the start of the 1958 revolution, Emad's father felt it was not safe to return to Iraq. He decided the family would stay in England and the children would go to school there until the political situation cleared. They ended up remaining in England because Iraq continued to be unstable, especially for the Kurds.

Emad visited Iraq twenty years later, in the late 1970s. Some Iraqis consider the 1970s as the "golden age" of Iraq. Education became public and free at all levels and was considered one of the best education systems in the region. Iraqi women enjoyed more freedoms than the women of neighboring countries. Saddam created a western-style secular legal system, making Iraq the only country in the Persian Gulf region not ruled according to traditional Islamic law, Sharia. His speeches in the 1970s contain many references to the "good Iraqi woman" being an educated, working woman. Policies were created to help women be successful, such as free childcare, transportation to and from work or school, and maternity benefits.

Emad enjoyed reconnecting with family and friends, so he revisited Iraq every few months. Each time he went, he could see the situation in the country going from bad to worse. The 1980s brought about the war with Iran, which, in turn, led to a diversion of public resources to military spending. The education budget suffered from a deficit, which continued to grow as Iraq's economy piled up a massive debt.

The 1990s were considered the crisis years, with the Gulf War and economic sanctions causing Iraq's educational institutions to decline even further. Education assumed only 8 percent of the total government budget, and the gender gap and dropout rate increased. The status of women under Saddam's rule then became worse. In an attempt to maintain legitimacy after the Gulf War and appease conservative patri-archal constituencies in Iraq, he began applying anti-woman legislation, such as the 1990 presidential decree granting im-munity to men who had committed "honor" crimes.

"It was desperation," Emad said. "The government was under the sanctions, but the people were paying for it. Young people who graduated from the university couldn't get a job as a street sweeper because nobody swept the streets. They couldn't do anything, so they became thieves or crooks or even committed murder to stay alive."

Murder was a rare thing up until the Gulf War, but a little less rare afterward. Maybe once or twice a year some-one would be caught for murder-robberies. When the killer was caught, the process was televised. The killer was filmed showing the Iraqi police how he committed the crime, like in one case where a man entered his neighbor's home and killed a mother and her two children. After he described each of his acts, he was hung in the same spot where he had killed them.

"The whole thing was wrong," Emad said. "It was wrong for the UN to sanction Iraq, and it was wrong for the Iraqi government to sanction its own people. The situation was very bad, and the only way to improve it was to get rid of the present government."

As I listened to Emad, I remembered my trip to Iraq, particularly the day Raad picked me up from my aunt's house. It was my last day in Iraq. My relatives and I shed tears as we kissed each other goodbye, a number of them telling me, "Don't forget about us." Relatives chased the van I was in, throwing water at it, a ritual that symbolized a wish for my return. *I will return one day*, I thought, *but not anytime soon.* I was tired of what I'd seen, of people needing this and that and suffering through one hardship after another. Their destitute attitude was a new phenomenon.

The Iraqis I had known before were of the 1970s era and famous for their reserved attitude, dignity, generosity, and hospitality. In post-war and UN-sanctioned Iraq, there were no stories of strength and inspiration, only of teachers selling baked goods in class or accepting bribes from wealthy students so that they could feed their own families. Or much, much worse, women resorting to prostitution and men turning to crime. One cousin told me how she sold her gold to buy a hospital bed, thread, and needle for when she delivered her baby. A mother with two daughters lamented about losing her husband, three sons, and the fiancé of one of her daughter's in the war.

One day the pedestrians of a busy main street stared distastefully at me and my cousins after we left a bakery with three large cakes. As we waited to find a taxi, one passer-by loathingly said, "I hope you drop the cakes on the floor."

"They haven't had cake for years," my cousin explained when she saw how disturbed I was at peoples' rudeness. "One cake costs an Iraqi one month's salary."

This was from a once developing country that not long ago was envied for its free health system, education and social programs, and its robust middle class.

Raad and I had a terrible journey out of Iraq. An hour

into the drive, our van broke down in the middle of the highway. With no cell or pay phones, the only alternative was to hitchhike. Many stopped to help but couldn't give us a lift because either they didn't have enough room in their car or they were not going as far as we needed to go, across the border. Some of the people who stopped offered to help fix the car, but I guess it was not a fixable problem. Eventually two men with an old lady picked us up. I sat in the back between Raad and the old woman for the next sixteen hours with nowhere to put my head but straight forward. My neck was stiff, my eyes burned with fatigue, and my nerves were in shambles as I prayed we would not miss our flight to America. Of course, we did miss it.

"We just crossed Iraq's border," the driver said.

I quickly looked behind me and saw the two dramatic white cement arches marking the Jordan-Iraq border. Between them was a sign that read, "The magnificent free Iraq bids you farewell and wishes peace upon you."

A dark cloud covered the whole region of this country, which was the size of California and sat on the map in the shape of a faceless lamb or tiger spread on the grass. The misery of war and sanctions were so heavy in the air that my lungs opened wide and my breathing improved once we were in Jordan, as if a Bedouin had appeared out of nowhere and served me a glass of oxygen, uttering with great compassion, "Here, young lady, you need this, given the isolated world you've come from."

The harder I looked in the direction of Iraq, the more I could not understand how man could exclude a country from the rest of the world when God had placed it there.

Mainly the UN, the US, and the UK collaborated to exclude a country from the rest of the world. They flat out and quite abruptly said to it, I am throwing your population of some twenty-six million into a monstrous insulated prison so that you cannot enjoy what you have been accustomed to enjoying for decades, centuries, even millenniums: the flavor of clean air and fresh water; the inventions of Benjamin Franklin and Thomas Edison so one could have a working refrigerator and air conditioner in the middle of 100-plus degree weather; the simplest advancements of medicine, like immunizations and ibuprofen, things that the rest of the world cannot stand to do without.

"The sanctions are a crime, a real honest-to-goodness crime," I had said to myself, feeling sorry that all I could really do at the time was recognize the crime, not stop it.

* * *

Around the year 2001, Emad signed a contract to supply Iraq with mobile communication equipment. "The communications in Iraq was totally bad," he said. "If you needed an ambulance, you could not call for an ambulance. There were no telephones, nothing."

Telecom communications equipment was on the list of the Oil-for-Food program, but contrary to how Darrin had described it, it was not as simple as filling out a two-page form. A supplier had to first go through an extensive process to get it. Dr. Nasi Abachi held two high government positions under the Saddam Hussein regime. He was head of the Frequency Management Department in the Ministry of Communications and head of the Mobile Department within the Iraqi Telecommunications and Postal Commission.

Dr. Abachi wrote letters on Dawn's behalf explaining what had happened between the Iraqi government and Emad. According to him, around 1996 or 1997, Alcatel, a company based in France, wanted to provide Iraq with the mobile network, but Alcatel never fulfilled the installation of the network because they were pressured by the US government to stay away from Iraq. In 2001, Saddam finally relented and agreed to let contractors bid on the installation of a mobile telecommunications network in Iraq. They signed contracts with eight companies. Of the eight, only one was able to get the job done. That was Advanced Technical Systems (ATS), Emad's company. Emad asked them to keep the project secret, which they figured was understandable as it was the only way Emad would be able to deliver the equipment without the US government intercepting.

Now that Emad had the deal, he had to supply. He contacted a number of companies in China, England, and India. He even visited people in Poland and Belgium. They all had certain parts, but the Iraqi government was after a whole system.

"If you know anything about mobile system, it is like a car without the fuel," Emad said. "The software is the most important of it, and that has to be installed by the manufacturer. So the equipment we were going to supply was technically not usable."

One day a man from the British Embassy called Emad and said he wanted to talk to him in person about his passport. Emad went to the Embassy and he was told, "We heard about your activities and we want to let you know that you are in danger. You shouldn't visit Iraq so much."

"I'm visiting Iraq with the permission of the British government," Emad said. "In one of our trips, Lord David Steel, presiding officer of the Scottish Parliament, and the Archbishop of Leicester came with us for a humanitarian visit. All of that is documented."

"Well, all right. But if we need you again, we will give you a call."

In Jordan a lot of people heard about the telecom deal and approached Emad, but he soon discovered that they were all talk. They could not deliver. Dawn's name was tipped to him and when he called her, he recognized that she had little knowledge about the telecommunication net- work and was not very up-to-date on how to obtain the equipment, but she was willing to try. That was her strong point. Six months after he contacted Dawn, the CIA got in touch with him.

"I was willing to cooperate with them for the sake of Iraq," he said. "I did not mind working with them, not at all."

Emad began to meet with CIA agents, two at a time and approximately four in number, on a regular basis until a few months before the invasion of Iraq in March 2003. They met in hotel rooms and cars in Amman, Jordan, where he was then living. They told Emad they wanted his cooperation to use the telecom equipment to track down Saddam Hussein and his military aides and listen in on certain conversations. They emphasized that they wanted his involvement to be kept secret for their own safety and his.

"Have you told your wife about our meetings?" one asked.

"No," Emad said.

They were pleased.

Emad was never offered payment nor did he ask for any. Money was not his main motivation. He knew that the only way to topple Saddam was to work from the inside. He'd wanted to do this for years. Unfortunately, all of those with information who he could have approached had left Iraq and started to exaggerate their knowledge and self-worth. Since he had spent most of his working life outside of Iraq, his contacts were limited to school friends. Undaunted, he began to build good relationships with new people and establish access to top personnel, even eventually to Saddam.

First he had to prove his loyalty to the Iraqi regime. He had to break the sanctions by supplying goods. There were already many people operating in spite of the sanctions and giving lucrative deals to their own friends – until Emad's company landed the mobile telecommunications deal.

"We had to act like we were pro-Iraq and wanted to totally bust the sanctions," Emad said. "We were given names of certain personnel that could help us along the way."

In September 2002, the agents provided Emad with names of Lebanese engineers who would work on the system and asked him to get visas for them, which he did. The agents visited him in his office in Amman, where he gave them the visas. They then established a company through contacts in Turkey.

"These contacts gave us maximum support to achieve our objectives," he said.

Once they formed the story about Turkey, everyone involved kept it up all the time so as not to let the truth slip in any way. "Technically, it was true that the goods were going to Turkey," Emad said, "which made it easier and believable to say so."

One of the agents who identified himself as "Jerry" met with Emad several times. Jerry told Emad, "We are not after you. We are not after anyone you are working with. Nobody will get hurt. Nothing will happen. We just want Saddam and his henchmen."

This was the green light for Emad to recruit Dawn, whom he kept in the dark, and his cousin, Kameran. Kameran, a man in his early sixties, was born in Baghdad. Between 2001 and 2003, he worked for Emad at the Baghdad office of ATS. Emad called him in December 2002 and asked that they meet in Amman, Jordan. Kameran flew to Amman on December 29. Emad met him at the airport, and on the ride into the city, he told him that they would be meeting with representatives of the CIA about the shipment of telecom equipment to Iraq.

"The Americans know all about the shipment," Emad told his cousin. "They want to ask you about the people you're dealing with in Iraq."

Kameran did not mind getting involved, and the next day, Emad and Kameran met with two American men at the Briston Hotel, an elegant hotel located in the center of the city. The two men did not identify what agency they worked for, but they confirmed that they knew about ATS's dealings with the Iraqi government. They showed Kameran copies of ATS's contract with the Iraqi Ministry and asked him questions about the Iraqi Military Industrial Commission and the Iraqi Technology Procurement Agency.

"If you give us the information we are after, we will help complete the telecom shipments," one of the men said, although he did not say exactly how. "After the invasion occurs, we will also help ATS secure a GSM (Global System for Mobile Communications) license and contract in Iraq."

Kameran agreed to their terms without pay as long as his safety was assured. "I want your word that the US will invade Iraq," he said, "so that Saddam's government cannot retaliate against me."

"Yes, this will happen," one of them said. "The US will invade Iraq."

"Give us an exact description of where you live in Baghdad," the other said, "so you and your family will be protected from the air raids."

They continued to meet a few more times, and then, on February 17, 2003, Kameran went to Damascus, Syria. The next day, at 3 am, Iraqi authorities broke into his home in Baghdad, attempting to arrest him. His family called and told him not to return to Iraq. Kameran then called Emad and asked, "Can you ask the Americans we met if they can help me?"

A week later, Kameran and Emad went to the Marriot Hotel in Amman, where they met with a third American, a woman who introduced herself as "Jenny" and said she was a colleague of the men he had previously met.

"I will help you," she said. She gave him a paper with

telephone numbers on it, one for her mobile and the other for her apartment in Jordan. Kameran met with "Jenny" again after the invasion and gave her a list of Iraqi officials' names, his friends, who should be recruited to cooperate with the new government.

"I want you to tell me which can be trusted and which cannot be trusted," she said.

He did his best. Between June and July of 2003, he helped arrange meetings between the American officials inside the Republic Palace and the Iraqi Air Force Commander as well as the Minister of Labor.

"Can you arrange a meeting with the chairman of the Iraqi Central Bank, Isam Huwaish?" she asked.

Kameran tried but was not able to because Isam Huwaish was missing at the time. Kameran kept in touch with "Jenny" on a regular basis after the invasion. In autumn 2013, she offered and encouraged him to take a position with the new government that was set up by the United States. He declined because he considered himself a businessman, not a politician. Still he continued to respond to her requests until November 2003, when "Jenny" told him that her work was done, so she would be returning to the United States. She wished him good luck and vanished.

"I think that the invasion of Iraq caused all my illnesses due to stress," Emad said. "I had high blood pressure. I became diabetic, and that triggered all the other illnesses I now have, which is almost crippling me."

The CIA agents were never able to provide special software for the mobile telecom system because the invasion came first. The equipment, still in boxes and untouched, was stored in large airport storage at the Baghdad International Airport, formerly Saddam International Airport, with all the US military mail, meals, and equipment.

After the war, Emad never went back to Iraq because of the security situation. The CIA asked him, "Are you going to Iraq?"

"No," he said. "Do you want me to be there for any reason?"

"No," they said.

That was the last contact he had with them. The government, who'd promised to give Emad the license for the telecommunication contract, then gave the license to somebody else. "I think they gave it to one of their CIA operatives in Iraq," he said. "So I was just used."

"Did they stop contacting you because you came out?" I asked.

"I have no idea. No idea. I did not follow up or anything because I was totally against the invasion."

"You were against the invasion?" I asked.

"Of course!"

"Did you express how you felt about the war?"

"Well, to a point where, at one stage, there was a wedding near Tikrit with the family of Saddam. And I was able, or I could have been able, to go to it. So I asked them if they could give me some sort of a device so that when I'm there I could indicate to them that Saddam is there and they could have blasted him away. The guy that I was talking to said, 'Well, if we do that, very likely it could affect you. It could kill you as well.' I said, 'Never mind, let's do that to save going to war.' But that idea died a natural death that nobody followed or cared about it."

"Hmmm." I sighed sadly. "Wow."

"They were not intending to get rid of Saddam. They were intending to go to war with Iraq. That's my feeling. And that's why after the war they couldn't care less about me or contact me or anything."

I remained quiet, still thinking of the possibility of not having gone to war.

"I have proof that the US's intentions were to cause a mess in Iraq," Emad said. "In one of the meetings with Madeline Albright, she brought in this fellow who spent all his life in Iran. He even had an Iranian accent. His name was Al-Hakim. At the meeting, myself and others said to her, 'What are you bringing this guy for? He's going to create a mess. He is in Iran's pockets and very much pro-Iran.' She said, 'We know what we are doing.' And of course they brought Al-Hakim in and he created mess and after he was killed, his brother comes in and makes a bigger mess," Emad said. "Albright was warned about it, but I think they knew what they were doing. They wanted to create a mess and they wanted to leave a mess. And that's what it is."

Mohammad Baqir Al-Hakim co-founded the modern Islamic political movement in Iraq in the 1960s. He was seen as dangerous by the ruling Baath regime because he worked closely with Iran's Ayatollahs. In 1980 he fled to Iran, where he created the Badr Brigade that fought alongside the Iranians during the Iran-Iraq war.

Madeline Albright was the first woman to become the US Secretary of State. She's currently a professor of Interna-

tional Relations at Georgetown University's Walsh School of
Foreign Service. In May 2012, she was awarded the Presi-
dential Medal of Freedom by US President Barack Obama.
In 1996, when asked on *60 Minutes* if the sanctions were
worth half a million children dying in Iraq, she answered,
"We think the price is worth it."

CHAPTER 14
The Deterioration of a Family

Aside from when she went to work, Dawn locked herself in her house for thirty days, lost thirty pounds, got seriously stressed out, then afterward began eating everything but the kitchen sink. Both she and her brother went to their respective doctors and got medication for anxiety and depression, though they tried to keep things positive in front of their mother. They told her that the attorneys were doing a good job of representing them, but didn't let her in on the details.

They didn't really need to say much for Linda to understand what was going on. It broke her heart to watch her adult son and daughter sleep in a fetal position due to stress. All she could do was pray, and pray, and pray.

Once Darrin and his sister were free on bond, Darrin's teaching at Oakland University was put on hold and his important missions were terminated. He moved into his mother's house to watch over her as best as he could. Linda also wanted her daughter to move back with her, but Dawn said no. She worried that her mother's health would be affected if she saw her in such an awful state. Linda made sure to see both Darrin and Dawn each day and to have someone close to Dawn stay with Dawn as much as possible during the night.

The Hannas were a tight-knit family. Linda and Toby's three grown children – Dean, Darrin, and Dawn – lived within a close proximity. Their father was born in Iraq as a Chaldean and their mother was American. Growing up, that was a bit odd for the children, as during the 70s and 80s it was somewhat uncommon for Iraqis and other Middle Easterners to have an American spouse. But because of this, Dean, Darrin, and Dawn had the best of both worlds. On Christmas, they ate ham and pacha – an Iraqi dish made from sheep's head, trotters, and stomach. They had grandparents who spoke no English and grandparents who spoke only English. They had loads of cousins, relatives, aunts, uncles, and second cousins from their dad's side, with only one uncle and no cousins from their mom's side.

Linda and Toby divorced when Dean was fourteen years old, Dawn was twelve, and Darrin was seven. Within a year, both found someone and remarried. Linda raised the children with her new husband, Rick. The children all agreed that he was a great stepdad and an awesome husband. Rick was American, had worked at Chrysler his whole life, was happy with his paycheck every two weeks, liked planning for retirement, and enjoyed family dinners. He married Linda when she had three kids, and he basically took them on as his own.

Dawn's father, Toby, saw the children regularly and kept the Chaldean culture alive in them as best he could. He felt it was important for them to know that their ancestors came from Ur of the Chaldees, which is reported to be the world's first city. Aside from being the birthplace of Prophet Abraham, it's likely the location of the famed Tower of Babel, today called the Ziggurat, which biblical accounts claim was built after the worldwide flood with the intent to have, according to Biblical accounts, "its top in the heavens...lest we be scattered abroad upon the face of the Earth."

Having worked at one point at the National Museum of Iraq, Toby was especially aware and appreciative of Mesopotamia's many historical sites, of the whalebone that hangs in the mosque of Nebi Yunis in the Nineveh Province, said to be a relic from the adventures of Jonah and the whale; of the gnarled old tree in the city of Basra, allegedly the one Adam and Eve ate the apple from, standing on the supposed Garden of Eden; of the Hanging Gardens, one of the seven wonders of the world, built by Babylonian king Nebuchadnezzar for his homesick wife.

After he and Linda divorced and he remarried, Toby had three children with his second wife, but he continued to be a good father to his first three because his motto was, "You never divorce your kids." He lived by these words. In the mid-1990s, he started Sunday's 10 am "breakfast club meetings" at Sero's, a Greek and American restaurant. As regulars at Sero's, Toby and his six children sat in the same booth for many years so that the waitress wouldn't screw up their order. God forbid someone forgot the toast, or gave them hash browns instead of French fries, or didn't have the coffee and pitcher of water ready when they sat down. If there was too much fat on his steak and eggs order, Toby would throw a silent fit, send it back, and demand to speak to the cook. The kids thought it hilarious and at times actually convinced their father to try something other than the usual breakfast special. To please them, he'd give in here and there, ordering a side Greek salad, gyro sandwich, pancakes, and even some rice pudding or tapioca for dessert.

Toby was happy to be surrounded by his six children, the three by his first marriage, who were now considered adults, and the three from his second marriage, who were half the age of their half-siblings. At first, the younger kids simply enjoyed eating their pancakes and getting a quarter for the giant circus gumball machine in the lobby of the restaurant. Later, they began to get involved in the conversations. Decisions were made about what hair dye color to use, which college to attend. Outfits worn by the teenage half-sister were approved or disapproved of. That same half-sister was once scolded for getting her belly-button pierced. And Toby got made fun of for his ventures: spending a small fortune to put a fish pond on his property; building a pull barn bigger than the house; and pretending he was living back in his birth village of Telkaif by planting a large radish and lettuce garden.

Darrin had even worked out an itinerary for the breakfast club meetings, which went something like this: old business discussions, new business discussions, general family concerns, and special requests. Then, at the end of breakfast, Toby grabbed the bill and everyone looked at him like, "Hi, we need some allowance here, gas money, shopping money, or pocket money." Toby would distribute cash to them for the week and off they went.

Emad had once joined them for Sunday breakfast at Sero's when he was in town. Toby was kind to all who came, but he was sometimes annoyed when the kids brought random people to the breakfast forum. He felt like it was their family time. To avoid upsetting him, his kids tried to get a mini-approval from him, and some people were actually denied access. Sunday's 10 am "breakfast club meetings" continued even when Toby went to Iraq as a translator. It came to a complete halt after the indictment, as Dawn and Darrin struggled with work and health issues.

While Darrin wrote a customized database program for the lawyers to help them in their research for the trial, Dawn helped him make flowcharts of timetables and projects for all the business activity involving TIGS. He complained to his sister, "You're spending too much time working instead of going through this mound of documents. You could be doing more."

"I don't want to dedicate my entire life to the trial," she said. "I can't afford anything anymore. I have to choose between making the house payment, keeping my phone, and paying for gas. We have to make money to survive, pay the lawyers, and keep the business going without having to sell everything we have on eBay."

Dawn had a lot of work going on with scrap metal trading and she was trying to maintain contact abroad with vendors while unable to travel. An associate in Germany did the best he could to keep his own business and their joint scrap metal business going, but even that became stressful.

Although Dawn had a good supplier, she'd learned that in the brokering business, if one was not present to see the material loaded up, it became really hard to maintain and manage deals.

Dawn was also dealing with a local guy in Trinidad who was loyal and trustworthy and aware of her struggles. She was on the phone with him at various times of the day, and they became good friends. After he ran around the island most days doing his full-time job and helping her, he would call her at about nine o'clock each night to recap where they were at. One night, Dawn took the call from Trinidad and about ten minutes into the conversation, everything became a blur. She was sitting on her couch in her TV room and she felt very dizzy. She tried to follow the conversation and talk, but her arm went numb and the room turned upside down. The guy on the other end of the line thought she was drunk because her words were slurred and she wasn't answering him properly.

"I don't feel well," she told him. "I got to go. I'll call you laaater…"

She heard him laughing, hung up the phone, and looked down the hallway. The armoire bar was turned upside down. She tried to focus on a piece of artwork and that was slanted too, as was the television set. Her phone rang and she saw from the caller ID that Trinidad was calling back, but she couldn't answer. She couldn't feel the left side of her body, so she crawled out of the living room, letting the phone ring. Finally, she called 911 but when they answered, Dawn couldn't say her name. She hung up, and the 911 operator called her back and asked if she needed an ambulance.

"No, well, I don't know," Dawn said.

They were on the phone for a short while, but it seemed like forever. She had a horrible headache, her body tingled, and she stayed lying on her living room floor. As she stared at the ceiling, she felt frozen, as though she was trapped in her body. When she felt good enough to get up, she talked to the 911 operator and said she was okay. Then she called her mother and noticed she couldn't hear very well out of her left ear.

On the weekend, she went for her usual spa trip and body wrap shop appointment. Her friend Marla looked at her and said, "Your face looks a little droopy."

Dawn told Marla what had happened. Another friend at the shop said that it sounded like she'd had a TIA, or a mini-stroke, like a pre-stroke but not as eventful. Marla suggested some electronic foot detox therapy. Forty-five minutes into the therapy, Dawn told her, "I feel my body and nerves kind of coming back."

Marla grabbed a mirror and held it in front of Dawn's face. "You look a little better."

When Dawn tried to smile, she noticed her mouth was still crooked. Marla gave her some essential herbs, homeopathic therapy and other remedies, and asked another friend, who was a minister, to come and pray with her and Dawn for this to pass. They did that and then encouraged Dawn to continue with the homeopathic therapy.

Dawn later went to her doctor, and he immediately said that what she went through sounded like a TIA from stress and anxiety. He sent her for an MRI and to a neurologist and told her to try to avoid stress so that this does not happen again. Dawn wondered how she could avoid stress when the government kept trying to settle the case with a plea bargain, otherwise threatening to indict her mother and father. She was tempted to take a plea and get this whole thing over with, to spare her parents from an indictment, but her attorney deterred her from doing so. He said that the government did not have enough proof to convict her. "And besides," he said, "in their plea they were asking for a ridiculous four- or five-year sentence."

The day Linda and Dawn were subpoenaed to go to the Customs' building and provide a handwriting sample, Linda decided to retain an attorney for herself. Then one day, as Dawn and Darrin sat with Linda's attorney in his Birmingham office, a voice mail came in from Prosecutor Barbara McQuade stating, "We are not planning to indict Linda at this time."

Although the family was relieved, they said to each other, "All this money that was spent and all of the fear and intimidation for nothing."

Laws governing private as well as public and political life were written up in Mesopotamia as early as 2250 BC. The oldest known law code surviving today is the Code of Ur-Nammu, King of Ur. There were several sets of laws found in Mesopotamia, such as the Code of Hammurabi, previously thought to have been the first law code until the discovery of the Code of Ur-Nammu. Hammurabi was the sixth king of Babylon. His code was inscribed on a stele and placed in a public place so that all could see it. A carving at the top of the stele portrays Hammurabi receiving the laws from the god Shamash or possibly Marduk. The preface states that

Hammurabi was chosen by the gods to bring the laws to his people.

The stele contained 282 laws, written by scribes on twelve tablets. The code is very precise, with each offense receiving a precise punishment. The punishment tended to be cruel by modern standards, with many offenses resulting in death, disfigurement, or the use of the "Eye for an eye, tooth for a tooth." The code is one of the earliest examples of the idea of presumption of innocence, and suggests that the accused and accuser have the opportunity to provide evidence. However, there is no provision for extenuating circumstances to alter the prescribed punishment.

I once asked the Red Indian how his people dealt with laws and such and he basically described it in similar ways to that of John Fire Lame Deer, a Lakota holy man who was quoted to have said:

> "Before our white brothers arrived to make us civilized men, we didn't have any kind of prison. Because of this, we had no delinquents. Without a prison, there can be no delinquents. We had no locks or keys and therefore among us there were no thieves. When someone was so poor that he couldn't afford a horse, a tent or a blanket, he would, in that case, receive it all as a gift. We were too uncivilized to give great importance to private property. We didn't know any kind of money and consequently, the value of a human being was not determined by his

wealth. We had no written laws laid down, no lawyers, no politicians, therefore we were not able to cheat and swindle one another. We were really in bad shape before the white men arrived and I don't know how to explain how we were able to manage without these fundamental things that, so they tell us, are so necessary for a civilized society."

CHAPTER 15
The Trial, the Verdict, the Sentencing

Jury selection began on September 9, 2008, even though Dawn's and Darrin's lawyers did all they could to move the trial away from the seven-year anniversary of 9/11. During opening statement, the prosecutor told the jurors that they would frequently hear the name Emad, an unindicted co-conspirator and the defendants' partner in this telecommunications deal.

"Now, there are some details in this case that we can't explain to you and can never explain to you," she said. "That is due in large part to the defendants' own efforts to conceal their illegal conduct."

The duty of the prosecutor is to seek justice, not merely to convict. Yet in the Hanna case, it seemed that the prosecutors tried to win the case at all costs. On the first day of trial, they asked for the Judge to instruct the jurors that the defendants, in order to be found guilty, did not have to know that what they were doing was illegal.

"Did they need to at least know there was an embargo against Iraq?" Judge Battani asked.

"I don't believe so," Prosecutor Michael Martin said.

"They don't have to know that? See, what is it they thought was illegal?"

"They could have thought it was illegal 'cause it violated the money laundering laws."

"So no knowledge of any illegality, is that what you're saying?"

"Yes. What we don't want is the court to instruct the jury that we have to prove beyond a reasonable doubt that Dawn knew about the embargo or any details about it or any details about regulations."

"The indictment alleges that they willfully and knowingly broke the law by shipping goods to Iraq," Dawn's attorney said.

"This is what they're accused of," Darrin's attorney said.

"May I respond to that?" Prosecutor McQuade asked. "This is a last minute attempt to make the burden on the government much higher than the law requires."

But in criminal cases, the burden of proof is placed on the prosecution, since they hold all the cards. They have unlimited resources, unlimited staff, unlimited time to prepare the case. Only by requiring proof of guilt can a citizen be partially protected from malicious prosecution. Without this constitutional law, it would be very easy for the government to round people they disagree with and put them in jail.

This need for the prosecutors to win continued on until the last day of deliberation, when a note came in from the jury that said, "If Darrin knew the deal was illegal on July 17, 2007, would he still be in violation of the laws in question?"

"I think the answer is clearly yes," Prosecutor McQuade said. "We have alleged that a conspiracy occurred between date x (December 2001) and a date y (July 18, 2007)."

"Your Honor, with all due respect to Ms. McQuade," Darrin's attorney said, "there's a difference between acquiring knowledge after the fact and being an active co-conspirator. If we look carefully at the counts in the indictment, there isn't an alleged crime charge that occurred beyond mid-2003. There was no testimony about events occurring in 2004, 2005, 2006, and 2007. I am troubled by this date that seems to be kind of artificially picked out of the air."

"It would seem to me that he would have to know at the time of one of the overt acts," the Judge said. "I mean, how could everything have occurred, and then he finds out, and then he's conspired?"

"Well, Your Honor, the law requires that one defendant commits an overt act in furtherance of the conspiracy," McQuade said. "But if he joined the conspiracy sometime within that window, that would be sufficient to satisfy the elements of the conspiracy." Later, she added, "I think the important point is that a conspiracy does not end until someone actively withdraws from it."

"But here it's different than withdrawing," the Judge said. "It's almost like they're asking somebody just getting into it."

"That's right," Dawn's attorney said. "You can't withdraw until you join."

"The indictment alleges that it occurred between December of 2001 and July 18…" McQuade began.

"I understand that," the Judge interrupted. "But I don't know how they would ever come to the conclusion he learned it specifically on July 17 'cause there was no evidence of that."

"I think the only reason the day ends up in there is because that's the date the matter was presented to the grand jury for their review," said Darrin's attorney. "There's no evidence."

Throughout the trial, there actually were no witnesses that testified against Darrin. There was hardly any evidence to prove he participated in a crime. On several occasions, Darrin's attorney tried to have the Judge dismiss Darrin's case.

That same day, at 3:45 pm, the court received a note from the jury that they had reached a verdict. The verdict was read by charge, in the following manner:

Count One, Conspiracy.

Dawn Hanna, guilty.

Darrin Hanna, not guilty.

The remainder of the verdict was read in the same manner, with Dawn being found guilty, Darrin not guilty. I once asked Darrin what it felt like to hear these words and he said, "It was like standing there and watching someone shoot your family. And you're just standing there, saying, you know, my sister just got shot. This is the worst day of my life. I guess for my family, at least they didn't shoot us both."

Judge Battani explained to Dawn that, in determining a sentence, she would consider the guidelines as well as Dawn's background, the circumstances of the crime, and what others would receive. These factors, she said, help in receiving a fair, equal treatment amongst defendants. The government then recommended a twenty-year prison sentence, which Dawn's attorney described as a "jaw-dropping, improper, and lopsided sentence."

Seven days before the sentencing, LaRene submitted a sentencing memorandum to Judge Battani. He wrote:

> Given that the government did not secure the indictment in this case for almost five years, Miss Hanna's efforts to defend herself against the charges had already consumed a goodly part of her young life. It's hard to fathom a twenty-year prison term for the export of used telecommunications equipment, which occurred approximately seven years ago, in violation of export sanctions, which came to an end within a few months along with the regime, against which those sanctions were established.

LaRene noted that according to the United States Sentencing Commission's own figures, in 2008, the median prison sentence for all offenders with a criminal history, including murder, was twenty-four months. In determining what constituted "just punishment," he provided a list from the US Department of Commerce Bureau of Industry and Security (BIS) of other similar cases, where administrative penalties far outnumbered criminal prosecutions. Even in criminal cases, usually probation or a fine or a combination of the two was imposed. In cases that did result in imprisonment, the median term was eighteen months and the mean term 30.2 months. Multi-year sentences were enforced typically in cases involving shipments of military equipment.

To help assist the court in making a fuller, more rounded appraisal of Dawn Hanna and the life she had led, LaRene submitted over thirty letters from family members, friends, neighbors, and business associates who implored the Judge to show leniency during sentencing. Almost all claimed that they were better persons and had richer lives as a result of having known Dawn.

LaRene also proposed for Dawn to do community service as part of whatever sentencing package the court ultimately deemed appropriate. Deacon Timothy Sullivan, the Chaplain for the US Department of Justice, Bureau of Alcohol, Tobacco, Firearms and Explosives, asked that the Judge allow Dawn to serve a two-year term under his direction, where she would help their organization provide aid to the thousands of people who rely on their support and services. In this two-year period, Dawn would not be permitted to earn any income and her time would be spent organizing food drives, handing out food and clothing, and assisting their staff with placement for the homeless, unemployed, children, and handicap. She would be responsible for fund raising for their new shelter development project.

"Personally, based on over thirty-nine years of experience as a special agent, deacon, counselor, teacher, and parent I don't feel it would benefit any side to put Dawn Hanna through the prison system or into incarceration," Deacon Timothy said. "There is plenty of work for Dawn here, as we would need her to expand our resources, assistance program, and volunteers."

These pleas or suggestions were evidently disregarded. On March 25, 2009, Dawn received a seventy-two-month sentence and $1.1 million fine, one of the harshest sentences for an export violation in history. In determining the sentencing, McQuade wanted to add a national security enhancement even though there was no evidence that Dawn's offense threatened the security of this nation.

"This was a very serious offense," McQuade said, "and although I don't think there's evidence to suggest that Miss Hanna was in any way seeking to put at risk the national security of the country, it does not require that the defendant knew that national security was actually affected. I'll also point out that the timing of this, coming just before the war with Iraq, makes it more than theoretical that this could have had an impact on national security."

So the national enhancement was added on.

Desperate to avoid prison, in mid-2009, Dawn contacted attorney Paul Rinaldi, who, in the end, swindled $131,000 out of her (he was later disbarred). When Dawn asked Rinaldi for her money back, he sent her to his buddy, a lawyer in Detroit. He said, "For $75,000, this lawyer could work a favorable deal for you."

Dawn recounted what took place at the meeting.

When she got there, this "buddy" suggested that he facilitate a meeting with the prosecutor who, at that time, he said, was seeking heavy support to obtain the US Attorney position in Detroit. "Something the government would like is that you give me some subject matter regarding Muslims and then you develop it into something that could be a case for them to prosecute," he said to Dawn. "Because you are seemingly intelligent, you have international contacts and have been in business, you could bring them what they want."

"So I would create cases for them?" she asked.

"Yes. Terrorist cases, but the government would give you a subject matter, a starting point. For example, a subject matter would be money laundering related to international business that the US Government could make a case and further develop."

"You want me to create something that is not there and make people commit a crime?"

"Well, you cooperate with the government and they cut you a deal."

Dawn was taken aback. This did not feel good, luring people into something that would otherwise not be something they would do. "I have to discuss it with my attorney," she said.

When LaRene heard about this proposition, he warned Dawn that if she pursued such a path, he would drop her. "I do not cut deals like this, and I don't believe in it," he said.

* * *

Dawn had to report to prison in Kentucky on September 9 by noon. The night before, she sat in her mother's home along with her father, uncle, brothers, and her boyfriend, a Jewish man known as "Little Darren" since he had the same name as Darrin. They tried to remain calm, and it was not so bad until the time came to leave. Linda was standing near the kitchen when Dawn broke down and grabbed her leg. "Please, Mom, please! Don't let me go!"

"It'll be okay, honey. I'll have you home as quick as I can."

Everyone told Dawn that she would not be in prison too long because the case would be sorted out soon enough. A lot of well-connected government figures were working on it. A maximum of one or two weeks and you'll be home, she was told. Linda handed her daughter a basketful of tears and promises before she let her go. Once Dawn, Darrin, Toby, and Darren were gone, Linda returned to the kitchen and prayed to the Dominican nuns card hanging on the kitchen wall. Dawn had gone to the Dominican nuns during the beginning of this ordeal and she got everyone a little prayer card.

"Please bring my daughter home as soon as possible," Linda pleaded, her hands clasped tightly and her head pressed against the wall.

Dawn's brother, father, and boyfriend drove her to the prison. They wouldn't let Linda come along, as they were afraid for her health. They called her often to let her know how Dawn was doing in the car and if they were able to keep her calm. It was a seven-hour drive. At the prison, Dawn was relieved to learn that she would be taken to the camp facility next door to the main prison. The main prison, which was for men, she later learned, sat behind barbed razor wire fencing and looked intimidating.

Her family had the opportunity to say goodbye and then the prison guard said that Dawn had to resume through the gates by herself. Feeling scared and overwhelmed, she walked into the receiving and discharge area, where she was fingerprinted, asked to take off all her clothes, and strip searched.

Her medical items were taken from her, and later she found out that, upon arrival, a paper was filed that said, "Discontinue all medical treatment, per Clancey." That was referring to Dr. Clancey, the medical doctor at the camp.

She was allowed to keep the cross she had on around her neck, but the diamond in it had to be removed first. The officer took a paperclip and popped the diamond out of the cross. It flung out and bounced, and they had to chase it across the floor. They sent it home to her mother along with her clothes. She was issued a beige uniform and blue canvas shoes and was placed in a cold cement cell, what felt like a cage, and sat there for several hours while the intake officers did her paperwork.

CHAPTER 16
CIA Operative's Fascinating Views

Autumn was here, adorning the tree leaves with copper, green, plum, and khaki hues. We only had evergreens in our background. The leaves stayed fresh and never changed color. The desk where I sat to write faced the backyard window, enabling me to look up every now and then, away from my computer screen, and watch squirrels climb the children's playground, come sniff food dropped on the wooden deck the day before, and bounce on tree branches as though they were on a trampoline. They were so adorable and sensible for not complicating their lives with a law-abiding lifestyle.

"You know, if I'm going to die soon, I want to die in peace," Emad said. "This is the only thing in my life that went wrong like that. She's the only person I know that went to jail directly because of my involvement."

As I listened to him, I drank my coffee and stared out the window, at the tree behind the neighboring brown house.

Two squirrels raced up the yule tree, and the whole thing shook like someone shaking the crumbs off of a tablecloth outside. Emad went on, explaining how he never mentioned to Dawn or anyone else that the equipment was going to Iraq because he would then have lost his cover. It was like going to the police and saying, "I want to rob a house." On several occasions the CIA people asked him if Dawn and Darrin knew of the real destination and he said, "No, definitely not." They kept asking. He kept saying, "No."

I talked to Emad about the "Dear Charles" letter that Agent Wallace found in TIGS's trash and used to obtain a search warrant. Charle, without the 's,' is the official name of this person, but everyone called him Charles because it was more natural to pronounce it as such: The letter said:

Dear Charle,

I would like to take this opportunity to thank you for your help and support in shipping our goods to Iraq via Syria. Your contacts in Syria were most helpful in shifting the goods speedily and promptly. Once again, our thanks and appreciations. Now we are working on another deal with the new administration there and expect that we will start shipping goods again. We will have to wait for the airport to open, and will revert to you as soon as we have something going. I understand that you have some of our money (from amount we overpaid initially) still with

you, and you are not prepared to refund as
you have been instructed on many occasions.
I would like to have your full and final views
on this.

Sincerely,
Walied Al-Aly

This letter was written by Emad. Charle owned a shipping company in England and, after Customs started investigating the telecom deal, he had a fallout with Emad and
Dawn. He owed them money which he refused to pay back,
so Emad came up with an idea to threaten him with this letter. When I asked Emad about the letter, he said, "What does
it have to do with Dawn? It was addressed to Charle, it was
signed by Walied from Dresser, and I wonder why Dawn left
a lot of rubbish on her computer anyway.'"

"Why do you think your efforts have not helped release
Dawn?" I asked.

"I have no idea. I really could not understand what they
get out of it. I really don't. The only thing that I suspect is
that what's his name, Brian Wallace, he spent two, three, four
years, I don't know how much time he spent on it, wasting all
that time, and probably his boss said to him, you know, 'You
better get something out of it or otherwise you're out on your
ass.' You know the way the American say things. And very
likely he did everything he could to make her guilty so he
looks big in front of his boss. That is the only possible reason
I could find. Otherwise there is no reason for it whatsoev-
er. Nothing commercial, nothing political, nothing financial.

Nothing, nothing, nothing. What do they gain by putting her in jail? It's not that the jails are empty and they want to put some people in it. It's overpopulated. So what is it?"

"There was a company, a much bigger company, you dealt with similarly to TIGS and that company also said they were duped by you, but they didn't get into as much trouble. They only ended up paying a fine."

"Yes, it is definitely a huge company. They supplied me with a communication disk, satellite disk, and microwave disk and things like that. It was a big order for them. They never suspected where it was going, and it was shipped to Jordan. And I think they said, 'Okay, we made a mistake,' and the government set a fine on them."

One piece of information that might have helped Dawn was not allowed to come in as evidence. A company by the name of Stratex entered into a contract remarkably similar to the contract that TIGS entered into and with the same people — ATS, Emad, and Dresser International, Walied Al Aly. The Department of Commerce challenged the exportation, suspecting that the goods delivered by Stratex were diverted to Iraq. Dawn's attorney explained that Emad would testify if called as a witness or by stipulation, that in fact the goods were diverted to Iraq. He wanted to call Otero as a witness to offer his opinion as chief of the legal services division of Stratex.

"Otero's opinion would be helpful to the jury," LaRene said, "because it demonstrates how a company much, much, much, much larger than these folks at TIGS would have innocently entered into exactly the same kind of transaction with exactly the same people and be duped by those same people into making a shipment, which had they known the true facts of, they never would have made. This evidence would show the capacity of Emad and his associates' ability to dupe the folks with whom they did business."

"Whether or not Stratex was duped by Emad does not tell you anything about whether Dawn and Darrin were duped by Emad," Prosecutor Michael Martin said. "They're just two totally separate things. There is no connection, and because there's no connection, there's no relevance."

"I think it is certainly relevant and helpful to the jury to know more and more information about the person by whom Dawn claims to have been fooled by," LaRene said. "I mean, if the person by whom I claim to have been fooled is naïve, that claim would be insubstantial. If that person turns out to be an experienced and accomplished fooler, then my claim to have been fooled gains weight."

"We have a large company, Stratex, and we have a small company, the defendants," said the Judge. "This to me in and of itself makes a big difference. I don't see the relevance, so I'm not going to allow that testimony."

"How come a big company pays a small fine and with me and Dawn they confiscated ten million dollars' worth of equipment?" Emad asked. "It was seized in London, and then it was gone. So I lost my money and I lost my country. And there was another company called Dresser International, and they were shipping to Iraq and all because the mother company of Dresser is owned by Dick Cheney."

Halliburton profited the most from the Iraq war, with $39.5 billion of US taxpayer's money.

"I know only one thing about Dick Cheney," he said. "I never trusted him. You know the funny thing about politics? All the people I don't trust, they seem to get elected. They must have some attraction to people. I think people like liars because they tell them all the lies they want to hear and people believe it. Like Bush, he said, 'Read my lips, no more taxes.' And six months later, he raised the taxes."

"I think people forget that…"

"No, people like to hear good things. They don't think that these people are liars. They think, oh, these people are going to give us a good life. They live a dream. You know when there was a recession, especially in England, they have bingo halls – I don't know what they have for the poor in the states – and all the small gambling increased. Going to the cinema increased because people went there to see a different life that would take them out of their misery. All this happens because people like to escape. But when they can't escape, they go and look for somebody else. They don't blame the master that promised them everything and didn't deliver. They can't. That's the trouble with politics."

The wooden chime produced an unusually loud sound. I looked up from my desk and saw a gust of wind blow the evergreens. Their firs swayed as their husks stood tall and still, like a woman with a long veil, the fabrics of her garment fluttering against harsh conditions but her body remaining strong and knowing. The squirrel who had been eating red berries off of the yew tree clung onto a branch, its tail wavering in the air like a flag.

Emad and I continued to talk about politics, about its contraries, like when Bill Clinton was nearly impeached for a private act that was no one's business, which was frivolous and embarrassing to air on television in front of the whole world while politicians that actually hurt and killed people did not even receive a slap on the hand.

The 9/11 Commission left many questions unanswered because of the initial destruction and removal of evidence and the budget being limited to $15 million, whereas $30 million was given to dig up the dirt in the Monica Lewinsky scandal. Of the 300,000 people Saddam was reported to have murdered, he was tried and hung for killing 148 men who'd first tried to kill him when George W. Bush, during his six years as governor of Texas, presided over 152 executions, the highest rate of any governor of American history. Saddam pardoned Kurdish men who fought with the enemy against Iraq, but Bush, with the exception of one serial killer, denied everyone, including a mentally retarded man and a great-grandmother. Why would he pardon a serial killer but not a great-grandmother?

"Dawn was put in prison for something she did not do, conspiracy and threatening national security," I said. "She might have committed an export violation, but that was based on an unjust law, the sanctions. The people that implemented the sanctions — none of them got hurt, most of them got rich."

"The funny thing is, they escaped it and blamed everything on the United Nations when the United States controls the United Nations. They said, 'Oh, he's breaking the UN law.' They think the United Nations is a friend of God on earth." He laughed. "It's not. The United Nations is another – I call it, uhhh, the whorehouse of the world, and the pimps are the Security Council. That's what the United Nations is." He paused. "Are you writing that down?"

"Yes."

"The sanctions against Iraq, who did it hurt? It hurt the poor people. The ones who suffer the quickest are the children. Half a million children got killed alone in the sanctions, and of course with the invasion, a million and a half got killed."

The figures, to be exact, are 200,000 Iraqis during the 1991 Gulf War; 1.4 million Iraqis during the 2003 war; 1.7 million Iraqis as a direct result of the sanctions. That's a total of 3.3 million Iraqis.

"The papers don't report about the sanctions," he said. "They just report about Saddam making weapons of mass destruction. They talk about that until the cows come home."

Emad thought certain restrictions during the sanctions were ridiculous, such as lead pencils. Lead pencils are called lead pencils but are not really made of graphite. One day somebody said, "Oh, graphite is used as nuclear reactor." But to create a nuclear reactor, one would need a hundred million pencils, stripped, to use the graphite in that manner. And even so, it would be too costly and impractical. "They just wanted to hurt the people deep down," he said.

"Why do you think the government chose you for this project?" I asked.

"I'm sure I'm not the only one. They have hundreds or more."

"I heard you have tribal ties to Saddam."

"I have tribal ties to half of Iraq. Saddam says he's related to me. I don't know how, but he said it. My uncle burned all the papers so that Saddam could not say we are related. From my mother's side, we are decedents of Ali, the cousin and son-in-law of Muhammad."

I went into the kitchen to refill my coffee. The smell of eggplant, cauliflower, and potatoes I'd baked in the oven the night before still lingered in the air. The house was quiet. Linda was taking the kids for a walk. She had returned on a few occasions to grab a blanket or a sippy cup, but otherwise, I had the house all to myself.

"You really put yourself out there by doing this," I said.

"Well, people do all sorts all sorts of things for their country," Emad said.

"I mean for Dawn. You coming out put you and your family in jeopardy."

"No, it's not really for Dawn. It's for the truth, and the truth should make some difference somewhere. I had hoped that justice would prevail in the United States of America, but in this case it did not. I mean, if Dawn was guilty, well, she's guilty; she took the chance. But she wasn't. I think that's really, really terrible. It's exactly what Saddam used to do to other people."

Emad told me about a friend of his whom he knew from school. He was married to an English girl. He went back to Iraq and worked under the secretary for the Ministry of Oil. He didn't like Saddam. He was pissed off during the Iraq/Iran war and talked against Saddam.

Saddam heard about it and the Iraqi government pretended he took bribes and they executed him. "So they pretend that Dawn did something and they put her in jail," Emad said. "Well, what's the difference? Put her in jail or executed her. The end result is the same. Maybe if they executed her it would have been more merciful instead of suffering everyday knowing she's innocent, which is more torturous than if she was guilty."

His voice was layered with such care and sadness that I now believed that Dawn did not know. The court trial was so one dimensional, with twelve witnesses or experts testifying against Dawn and she the only one defending herself, that when reading the transcripts there was doubt whether she was telling the truth. Not that that mattered, really. This story was a lot bigger than answering the question, "Did she know?" This story was about the bigger questions and answers, which our lives and the lives of our children and the survival of our earth depended on.

"I really truly think the US behaved like a third world country," Emad said. "No difference at all from what the US is doing and what Saddam was doing. So all that war, all that pretense to get rid of a dictator who did a lot of injustice to his people, and it [the USA] is doing the same thing but with what you call the freedom and democracy of the US. It's a myth. It's really a myth. If they don't like you, they get you. The law and justice does not help you. It doesn't exist. It only exists if you have a traffic violation."

When Linda and I thanked Emad for participating in the interviews, he responded, "You all are welcome. Let us hope that Dawn's luck will change and the US becomes the land of the free once again."

CHAPTER 17
Prison Life

Saturday, November 27, 2010, 8:25:21 PM

I was fighting for a pork chop a few nights ago because the officer in the food service area decided to tell the servers to only give us small portions. It was sad and pathetic to see. About 15 to 20 inmates came in late. They were hungry and he said "No seconds!" The cafeteria only seats 44 people and there are 300 inmates. You can do the math. Rumor then had it from what we call inmates.com that he threw the food away. Food is thrown out constantly. One guy won't even give us an extra piece of bread, let alone leftovers. He freezes them or puts them away for the next day. He acts like it's his food and he paid for it.

I haven't had a pork chop in two years, so I was actually looking forward to it. However, the one server doesn't like me so I always get blackened, burnt, or small pieces of meat (somehow she always seems to serve the main dish or at least grab my tray when I go through the line). Some people do not like me because of two words: Arab and money. They feel and they have told other inmates, "That bitch got it, she don't need nothing. We will give her small portions." It's a racial thing.

I got 10 extra French fries yesterday from a nice server and ohhhh! Haters! Over a few extra French fries, I got called "A fucking bitch – got all them fries." Are you serious? Freedom or French fries? Please. That's what prison does to people, though. The Feds take everything away from people and when they get here, they are bitter, nasty, and hateful. It's literally inhumane inside this prison, how people beg for milk and other things to try to stay healthy.

Here we are considered sub-human, animals. We get cussed at by some officers, referred to as "crazy ass bitches." I love the constant reminder by staff when they bust out and say, "Ya-all put yourselves here, we/I didn't" or "Ya-all broke the law, we didn't." I just think, "Wow! I guess the Government is perfect and never makes mistakes?" Funny thing is the Government always breaks the law.

Yeah, your tax dollars at work baby! That's what Ya'all are paying for!

Regards,
Dawn

There were no tissues in reach, so I dried my tears with the back of my hands. Then more tears poured forth. This time I used my sleeves. I tucked my eyes into my palms and mourned the idea that over 300 women were placed in a facility that holds less than 200, that some of these women had left their babies behind or were past the age of 80 and disabled. None had committed violent crimes, all suffered some type of health issues, and most fought over or provided sexual favors in exchange for a bag of chips or cookies.

My refrigerator was still stacked with leftovers from the Thanksgiving we celebrated two days ago, a third of which was probably going to end up in the garbage. My family and I had slept in a warm bed while the women in Dawn's prison slept on steel framed beds with four-inch plastic-covered mattresses, hard as concrete, uneven and cold. Dawn had the top bunk bed and used a plastic chair to climb up and down. When she got out of bed, she fell down most mornings because she had back problems. She asked for a bottom bunk pass and was told she could not get one. She would have to use two chairs to climb up.

The prison building was filled with asbestos and lead paint, she told me. The women received little or no sunlight during the days. Sleep was disrupted with four head counts; at 10 pm, midnight, 3 am, and then 5 am. Officers flashed bright lights into each woman's face and carried on a conversation while turning up their radios, the CBs. The broken sleep made it difficult for the inmates to function during the day. The inmates lined up once a week for toilet paper, pads, and tampons. If the prison was out of toilet paper, they had to share a roll. Dawn's mother was able to send her money to buy shampoo, toothpaste, soap, and other hygiene items so that she didn't have to worry as much as the other inmates did about these items running out.

The stories Dawn sent me from prison reminded me of scenes from *Midnight Express* – without the violence, but with the same idea, "man's inhumanity to man," as the director and writer of *Midnight Express* described it. *Midnight Express* is a movie about Billy Hayes, a young American sent to a Turkish prison for trying to smuggle hashish out of Turkey and his family's attempts to free him. The story was originally a book that was adapted into a screenplay by Oliver Stone. The movie, which ended up winning six Oscars, created a lot of controversy because it had deviated from the book's accounts of the story. Both Stone and Hayes expressed their regret about how Turkish people were portrayed in the movie. Stone even apologized for "tampering with the truth."

I minimized the Corrlinks website and checked my inbox.

The phone rang, startling me. It was Linda.

"Did you get the email I sent you?" she asked.

"I'm actually checking my emails right now."

"Can you read what it says?"

Linda had copied and pasted a comment someone had posted online on the Oakland Press website. The newspaper had published an article a few weeks prior about the documentary we were making and the status on Dawn's case. The story got front coverage with a photo of Dawn's family and friends huddled together over a computer.

"I see about three or four things wrong with this family's story," I read the message aloud. "First, she was found guilty on all six counts! Conspiracy is very difficult to prove. You have to have two parties to complete the conspiracy, so someone testified. That entire group of people in that photo better be on a government watchlist somewhere because where there's one terrorist, there are twelve." I lowered my voice. "She should have gotten life."

"Sometimes, Weam, I just don't know," she said. "I try to keep it together and then I figure, screw it. Nothing is going to work."

"I wouldn't take this too personally. It's one guy basing his opinion on opinions."

"It's not one guy. It's a sign of our times."

"We have a load of work, Linda. Are you going to let this little thing bring you down?"

She sniffled. "No."

"What time are you coming over tonight?"

"Whatever is good for you," she said. "And don't cook! I'm bringing stuffed cabbage. I was up all last night making it."

"But I wanted to try out my Indian dish on you."

She laughed. "Next time."

"And don't bring anything for the kids!" I warned, since

she never came over empty handed. The doorbell would ring and my children would rush to the front door, dancing to the tune of "Aunt Linga is here." Linda would walk in with what my son called a "purprise," environmental bags filled to the brim with goodies — food, dollar-store items, and toys that ranged from an indoor tent to Dora and SpongeBob blankets — which made my children feel as though I'd become friends with Mrs. Santa Claus.

The next couple of days were spent preparing for Dawn's birthday/fundraiser party, which was to be held on Tuesday, November 30. The Hanna family decided to put together this event in order to bring awareness to Dawn's plight and raise money for the family's legal fees. I was part of nearly every decision – the location, the guest list, the invitations – while playing advocacy by calling Amnesty, Code Pink, and the UCLA. I went to Linda's work to meet with the volunteers. Linda played with the kids while the volunteers and I discussed how we were going to sell the 1933 Ford Victoria that belonged to Linda's now deceased husband.

"He bought the Vicky in New Jersey," Linda said, placing my son on her lap and feeding him ice cream, "during a family vacation to Pennsylvania. We followed him home." She laughed. "With him driving his new chopped rod, it looked like a scene from *Bonnie and Clyde*."

"There's this online company where we can auction the car," one of the volunteers said.

"How about if we auction it right there at the party?" someone else asked.

"Maybe have it sit in the parking lot?" another person

suggested.

Linda shrugged. "We can do that."

I could see from Linda's awkward smile and teary eyes how much selling the car saddened her. She had told me how Rick had customized it to his perfect standards. They had many fun times with the Vicky. They went to car shows and won ribbons, to Cruise Nights at local places, had taken the kids and their dog, Nicole, for a ride to get ice cream, or simply tooled around downtown Rochester. At the funeral home where Rick was placed, which Linda's family had used for decades, a beautiful area in the front of the entrance door was cleared and Rick's friends parked the Vicky there with pictures and his cruise hat.

"Are you okay?" I asked Linda.

"I just hope that my daughter will come home soon, back to the home full of memories, peace, and love," she said. "It's the only thing I have left."

One of the girls walked into the conference room and said, "Dawn's on the phone."

Linda looked at me like she was at her wit's end, so I offered to take the call.

"Just press line three," the girl instructed and then walked out again.

"Hi, Dawn," I said. "How are you? Tomorrow you're turning thirty-eight."

"Oh my God, I feel so good! I even got up this morning to work out at five." She laughed. "My friend Rebecca set my alarm with snooze every four minutes, pissed off the entire room. She said she wanted to make sure I got up and went to the gym with her."

"Wow, the gym this morning, yoga the other day. Luxuries I don't even have."

"Please, the gym is like the size of your garage."

"That's not the point. I can't even get to the gym because I'm stuck behind the damn computer working on your story."

"Don't worry. Once I'm out, I'll babysit your kids so you can get to the gym."

"Yeah, right. I'm sure that's one of the first things on your list of what you'll be doing once you're out of prison."

"Well, to be honest, when we talk on the phone, their yelling in the background scares the shit out of me. What on earth do you feed them?"

"Typical Chaldean food."

"Oooh," she cried. "I'm dreaming of pacha! Pacha for Christmas."

"I'm not that advanced that I know how to make pacha. Your mom will do that. But I'll make you a pot of dolma."

"Oh Weam, it feels so good to laugh. I do think, and hope, that this is all coming to an end finally."

"You have one minute remaining for this call," the automated voice said.

When the call ended, I turned around and saw my son had chocolate all over his face and shirt. In an effort to avoid thinking about the work that awaited me at home, I asked Linda if I could use her computer to check my emails. She led me to her office. I logged onto my email account and saw an invitation for tomorrow. Bishop Ibrahim was doing a presentation on his visit with the Christian refugees in Syria, Lebanon, and Jordan. The next email was from Issa, the LA producer. He wrote, "Hi, Weam. Hope all is well. Just wanted to say hello and let you know that I'm in Dearborn. I hope to lock the Bugliosi picture ASAP."

I sent him an invite to Dawn's event, and he said he would be coming with his business partner, Salem.

The event was held at the Corner Cigar Bar. A live band volunteered to sing, and Linda brought the food and two huge cakes. Bill Proctor, an investigative reporter for Channel 7, came to cover the event. We were very excited. Proctor had been working for WXYZ for over twenty-five years and was an influential figure in the community.

"I'm very glad to see you've come so far with this project," Issa said.

"Thank you."

Issa stood next to his partner Salem. He was in jeans and a winter jacket. He had on a black cap, which was placed backwards on his head. He had a long Arab/Jewish nose and his eyes appeared to be wide open, like a deer in headlights.

"Hey, where's Dawn's brother, the guy people call a 'genius'?"

"Oh, he's upstairs with Bill Proctor, a famous local reporter for Channel 7."

"That's great, Weam! Everything seems to be running smooth, isn't it?"

"Not exactly. We haven't raised half the funds we need to complete the documentary."

"That's surprising. I know that there's a tremendous Arab and Chaldean community here. I was actually hoping that you can introduce me to a few. If not, no worries, just thought I'd ask."

"There is a tremendous community here, but they have not been supportive. They rarely are when it comes to the arts."

"Ever hate being part of the Arab community?" he said, laughing. "The old saying keeps ringing in my head: 'Arabs never miss an opportunity to miss an opportunity.'"

"The funny thing is that they sit with us and listen to what we have to say and seem sincerely interested, but then nothing."

"Yeah, they almost give you a standing ovation, don't they?"

"Besides, it's not easy for me to get to these meetings. I have two young kids, and when I go through the trouble of having someone watch them, then go sit with people and talk and talk and talk about the same thing – the project, Iraq, the Arab world – it gets old and tiring."

"Didn't you have this one woman helping you out? Think her name was Bonnie?"

I nearly choked on my coffee. "My God this is the second time her name was brought up today. I hope she doesn't suddenly pop up here."

"What, you guys had a falling out?"

"She's crazy."

"I thought she brought a lot of people to the table?"

"They were my contacts! And in the end, we didn't close a single deal."

"It sounds like this girl was a good bait and just needed someone to know how to take the hook off the fish once it was caught."

"What?"

"Look, you once said that this girl is very passionate and relentless about getting what she wants, right?"

"Yes."

"Well, that's a great asset in a producer."

"But she never got anything accomplished. Plus, she got me into trouble."

"How so?"

I was quiet. "I can't explain it right now, but I just can't deal with her again."

"Then let me do it."

I looked at him in astonishment.

"Weam, I can help you with this case and the documentary. In order for Dawn's story to make a difference, Dawn must win the appeal. Otherwise, none of this will count. To do this, you need the right people and a lot of people. You also need the funding."

The cinematographer came to talk to me, and I excused myself. I returned ten minutes later. "How about we meet later this week?" I asked him.

"We'd be honored!"

Salem, who had white hair and wore glasses, smiled wide. He had not said more than a word or two the whole time. He was a quiet man with a humble air about him.

"Dawn will be calling any minute," the production manager said. "We'll be doing the cake now."

"All right, I'm coming," I said, smiling about the speech Dawn was going to give over the phone. I wrote it because she'd been too busy cleaning bathrooms.

CHAPTER 18
A Possible Happy Ending

"It's strange. My best friend in here is walking around sad, and I seem to finally be happy, working out again, eating, cooking," Dawn said. It was the morning of December 1st, the day after the birthday/fundraiser event. "So I asked her why are you so sad and pissy, and she said, 'Dawn, your journey is over. You goin' home, girrrrl.' I said, 'Why did I come here?' And she said, 'Me. You came to meet me, and now I know I can make it and I just feel sad.'"

"When I read your letters or listen to you talk, I go into a totally different world," I said. "I learn so much and become double appreciative of everything around me. I can't wait to meet you in person."

"Yes, I am such a lovable and awesome person!"

The energy of this project was like a bird whispering positive messages into the ears of the inmates, but what if this positivity ended up making little or no difference? Or worse, what if it was destructive in that it crushed peoples' hopes and desires? Whatever it did or did not do, by now it was too late to turn back. Besides, this story pursued me. Like an eagle after its prey, it covered me with its wings as it dove into my territory.

"So, did you celebrate your birthday last night? How does it feel to turn thirty-eight?"

"Celebrated my birthday? Uhmmm, no. Actually, holidays are so depressing in here, and the real punishment is for my family. The mindset of the government is destructive to families. You would most likely lose your husband while you're here and your kids may not know you. Some women left newborns with their mom or sister and most have at least a two- to eight-year probation, which is prison on paper, and if you screw up, at the discretion of the government of course, yup, it's back to jail again. So it's a system that can hem you up for life because it is a business!"

I did not know what to say to that.

"I'm at a work camp. That's all it is."

I still did not know what to say.

"Sorry, back to my birthday. I feel like I'm wasting years, and it's not really something I want to celebrate. It's the other inmates that try to make it special. They contribute with food, and we all eat together and reminisce about the free world. I've learned a lot from these women. My life seems exciting to them." She was quiet. "Weam, do you think I'll be home for Christmas?"

I hated that question. She asked it a lot, and I honestly did not have an answer for her. I didn't want to lie to her, an adult, when I was not the type that lied to children, not even about Santa Claus and tooth fairies.

"So what did you use for cake?" I asked her to change the subject. "Ding Dongs from commissary?"

She cracked up. "No! They made an Oreo cookie cake for me. Today it will be a cheesecake."

"You guys are really fancy in there."

"The Oreo cookie cake was great, fattening as hell, but I ate it. I'm no longer picky, and so my stomach is swollen to where I look like I'm ready to deliver an eight-pound baby most of the time, but hey…in the spirit of breaking down a human being, I'm in prison. I've lost weight, though, so I hide my Atwood Baby well."

"What's an Atwood Baby?"

"You know, Atwood Camp, baby belly from the sodium in all the food."

We laughed.

"How do I feel about turning thirty-eight?" she said, turning serious. "Well, I feel like the government took all my thirties away from me. I sometimes wonder how the prosecutors sleep at night. I can only hope for karma…"

"You have one minute remaining for this call…"

"Anyway, I hope you guys had fun at *my* birthday party last night – without me. Did you take a balloon home for me like I asked you to?"

The phone disconnected, and I barely had a chance to glance out the window before it rang again. It was Issa. He mentioned Bonnie again and tried to convince me that bringing her on board would be great for the project. I explained, again, that she was crazy and could not close a deal, to which he said, "But I can close a deal! Look, all this girl needs is someone to help her focus and give her direction."

How can I convince him that this woman is insane? I wondered, remembering the last time I saw Bonnie, when she told me that she had been revirginized thanks to a costly surgery. I told him I'd think it over, and we decided to meet at Panera Bread with Dawn's family to discuss the possibility of him working on Dawn's case. Before anything, he wanted to know a little more about Dawn's ex best friend who testified against Dawn. I will call her Ava.

Dawn met Ava when she was seventeen years old, in her first year of college. They became fast friends even though they were different in many ways. Ava had bleached blonde hair and Dawn was a dark brunette. Dawn lived on the campus and was completely dedicated to her studies. Ava lived in the basement of her Polish boyfriend's house and she had two jobs. Ava was always in a hurry for everything because her life was chaotic. She often joked about living out of her little red Ford Escort. Her parents were divorced, and her father lived in another state.

Dawn's stepdad, Rick, on the other hand, was very involved in Dawn's life. He brought along his friends to install her dorm carpeting, a phone jack, all the electronics, mirrors, shelving, and a refrigerator so that Dawn's dorm would look like a small apartment. His office at Chrysler was nearby, so he would go to Mercy College for a visit, or Dawn would invite him, with the meal tickets that were included in her scholarship, to lunch at the college cafeteria.

One of their classes ended at 10:40 pm, so Ava, feeling exhausted, would often ask Dawn if she could stay at her dorm. Even though the nuns discouraged guests crashing at the dorm, Dawn allowed it. Ava would then bring over White Castle with a five dollar bottle of white zinfandel and they would stay up studying and talking. Dawn didn't mind being Ava's friend, but she remembered how when Ava introduced her to her boyfriend, she'd said, "This is my first Arab friend."

Dawn didn't think much of it at the time, didn't pay attention to racial profiling, but later recalled how Ava had said she would never befriend Chaldeans, who drove new cars, wore nice clothes, and were very stuck-up. What really annoyed Ava was when Chaldeans pulled up to Little Caesars, where she worked, and paid for a $1 slice of pizza with a $100 bill. "But you, Dawn, have a little more class and you're more on the nerdy side, so you don't act like the typical Arab."

Dawn and Ava were best friends up until 2005. Dawn was even a bridesmaid at Ava's Renaissance-themed wedding. Dawn had bought a Stevie Nicks-style dress from a catalog called Wizards and Witches. Although the groom was Polish, the groomsmen wore Scottish kilts. It was a noontime wedding with a buffet-style breakfast of eggs Benedict and pancakes. It was the first time Dawn saw Ava's mother. When Ava and her bridesmaids were getting ready, her mother came in loud, wearing a silver sequence dress and a red sequence hat. She later commanded the dance floor with her third husband as he swirled her around and around. Darrin, Dawn's parents, and their spouses also attended the wedding because they really treated Ava like what Dawn described as a "blonde-haired step-child." They invited her to Chaldean dinner events despite her over-opinionated comments. She always went toe-to-toe with Toby about the Arab culture and how underpowered their women were.

It was not long before Ava got a divorce, and in 2003, she decided it was time for the Lord to be in her life. She joined a church and said it was a place to meet "good Christian" people who had good morals. "Unlike you, Dawn."

In court, Ava claimed that Dawn told her she was trying to get a communications system set up in Iraq. So she asked Dawn, "How will you get this equipment through to Iraq if there's an embargo?" In response, Dawn allegedly made a comment that it would go through Turkey first before it went into Iraq. Ava said that her friendship with Dawn ended because they just drifted apart. Dawn was very busy; she was constantly traveling, constantly working. Also, she felt she wasn't going down the same path Dawn was in life.

"What do you mean by that?" Prosecutor Michael Martin asked.

"For pretty much ultimately what we're here for today," Ava said. "I didn't agree with what she was doing. It's against our country policy. It's because I'm a patriot."

"And yet it took you three years to break off your friendship with Miss Hanna?" Dawn's attorney asked during cross-examination.

"I don't know the time frame, how many years or whatever," she said.

"You learned before you went with Dawn to London in 2002 that Miss Hanna was involved in this criminal activity that you so horribly deplored. Yet not only did you not break off your friendship, but you went on a trip with her. She paid for your ticket and you stayed at her flat. You even went to work with her at her brother's company, didn't you?"

"I didn't work with Dawn. After I left Cingular, I went to TIGS on a daily basis, as I was looking for a job. I felt it would be easier to look for a job in an office environment instead of sitting home."

Dawn's attorney brought, as evidence, Ava's resume, despite the prosecutor's several objections that it was "hearsay." In the resume, under career history, she wrote that she worked for over a year at TIGS as a sales consultant. Ava did not dispute what was written in her resume, her only defense being, "I don't remember the time frame." This became the basis for much of the rest of Ava's testimony. The attorney showed her various emails where, between 2004 and 2005, Ava invited Dawn to parties, like the adult Easter egg coloring party she threw. She sent Dawn information about health matters, heartburn, and Weight Watchers. She had gone to her stepdad's funeral, had lunch with Dawn at Champs in August, called her repeatedly, and invited her to a purse party. She continued communications with her just five months before she appeared in front of the grand jury in February 2007. Yet she told the grand jury she hadn't had contact with Dawn for years.

"You sent an invitation on September 16, 2006, to a bunch of folks, including Dawn Hanna, correct?" LaRene asked.

"I was trying to get as many people as I could to the purse party 'cause you get a gift."

"Including international criminals."

"She was not an international criminal at that time."

"She had become one, however, by February 2, 2007,

when you spoke to Special Agent Wallace."

"No."

"When you testified before the grand jury five months later you said that you had not seen Dawn or talked to her in a couple of years."

"That was just my best guess."

Ava not only had a terrible memory, but she went and volunteered to Special Agent Brian Wallace that Dawn was dealing with uranium. In actuality, it was urea, agriculture fertilizer for farming, which Dawn was trying to send to Bangladesh.

"That's the best friend that testified against Dawn?" Issa asked.

We were at Panera Bread with Salem, Linda, and "Little Darren".

"What a crock of – excuse my language – shit! She repeatedly flip flops, and yet she's called a witness? A witness to what? The world of bigotry and delusions? She tells the grand jury, 'Oh, oh, I haven't seen this horrible criminal for years!' when she went and had lunch with Dawn just six months before that. She puts TIGS as an employer on her resume, yet says, 'Oh, oh, I was just typing a few letters on their computer keyboard! I wasn't even using my fingertips, just my nails.' Well, if she has amnesia half the time, what is she doing giving testimony that could ruin someone's life? And what's with the prosecutors calling a resume, which she created herself, hearsay?"

"Dawn was basically doomed from the start, when the government insisted to have the trial bull's eye with the seven-year anniversary of 9/11," Little Darren said. Darren was clean-cut, well-built, with a dark complexion, light green eyes, and perfect teeth. Dawn met Darren in 2005, when he was working at his family business, which was dedicated to precious metals, and coaching wrestling and football at the Temple of Israel. At the time, he was also trying to get his teaching certificate. He had already failed the test twice. Dawn helped him study, and the third time he took it, he passed. He since called her his "good luck charm." With his teaching certificate, Darren began to teach third grade Hebrew at the Temple of Israel.

"Whoever attended this trial said the case was confusing as hell and that the atmosphere was like that of a terrorism trial," Linda said. "They put all the family's pictures up there on the screen, including Najib, who looks like a terrorist."

In Court, the prosecutors wanted Stan, a former employee at TIGS, to testify that he had heard Dawn talk about sending firearms to the Middle East. The defense pointed out that Stan's testimony might create a racial prejudice outcome. The Jordanian police force requested from Dawn a quotation for small arms, rifles, and pistols for a program that was funded by the US. Therefore, the Jordanian police force preferred American and British vendors, like Bushmaster, so that the money went back into the US economy. The transactions had nothing to do with Iraq and the Hannas never got the deal. Dawn's attorney said, "Even though this deal was entirely legitimate, legal, and ultimately unconsummated, the image of the Hannas as arms traders to the war-torn Middle East carries with it a potentially dangerous and prejudicial type of allegation."

"Is there any way to talk about what happened without discussing the guns?" the Judge asked.

"It would be very difficult," Prosecutor Martin said. "The persuasiveness of the testimony would be seriously diminished. And I might also add that any prejudice that may come out as a result of the testimony could be *cured* with an instruction. I don't mind if the court instructs the jury that they're not on trial for exporting firearms."

"Quite frankly, I don't understand why the testimony could not be sanitized," Dawn's attorney said. "The only reason I can think of to get very specific is because they want to wave the guns in front of the jury."

"This is a hard issue because of the world situation with Iraq," the Judge said. 'But I do not think it is more prejudicial than probative. Therefore the court will allow the testimony.'

"They not only brought up the firearms," Little Darren said, "but they highlighted them so bad, the word Bushmaster M16A2 kept ringing in our ears."

"This whole case is bullshit," Linda said. "It's all about covering up the $43 million that the government used illegally on this project. This one guy involved in the telecom deal, he said he couldn't come testify because the government threatened with his citizenship, told Dawn, 'If you dig deep enough and follow the money, you'll find out the truth.'"

"This is unbelievable!" Issa said.

"The first thing Bill Proctor said is that Dawn is being profiled and that our family has been targeted," Linda said.

"Well, that's apparent," Issa said. "Your reporter is holding the government accountable. This is where your participation makes a difference."

Linda looked straight at him, her hand in prayer form and pressed beneath her breasts, something she did often when anxious and scared, which made her look like a little girl. "Issa, can you help?"

"Because we are broadcasters and journalists, we can have sealed documents unsealed," he said. "Linda, please rest assured that based on the current evidence in hand, those involved in this case will not only be removed from office, but you can also have them disbarred, criminally prosecuted, and held liable for gross misconduct."

Linda took in a deep breath, smiling.

"Please allow me the ramp-up time to establish a stable team that will help implement our overall strategy. Once we're able to, we'll be demanding, in mass numbers if need be, an immediate submission for a Motion of the United States to set aside the verdict and dismiss the indictment with prejudice."

Raising her eyes with excitement, Linda squirmed in her seat.

"There are a lot of people and organizations that need to be brought on board the Free Dawn Hanna project. I might – I'm not promising – but I might be able to get Vincent Bugliosi and Richard Fine on board." He looked at me. "Weam, you know who Richard Fine is, don't you?"

"Yes, you sent me many links about him."

"Richard fine, a seventy-year-old attorney, was held in solitary confinement at a Los Angeles County jail for fourteen months even though he was never charged with a crime," Issa said. "He called himself a political prisoner. What happened is that he took on the corruption of the courts, and in return, they put him in prison! But people were not willing to stand for that. They raised hell, and guess what? A few months ago, he was released."

Everyone listened intently, as if they were sitting in a classroom or movie theater.

"Synchronization of all the key elements is extremely vital if we plan on beating the odds and forcing Dawn's immediate release and compensation," he said.

Linda started crying.

"Here you have example kids with PhDs," he said. "Dawn is a role model, and I would adore it if my daughter were to follow in her footsteps. What the government did is unethical and borderline illegal, and it's not American. I'm passionate about this subject because I love America so much. It has the best justice system in the world. Look, in Syria if you go up the hill and get stuck, people laugh at you. In America, they send a whole army to get you. In Syria, if you get into a car accident and you are Christian, you'd best read your last rites."

We chuckled.

"Linda, as much as I'd like to, I can't and won't promise you anything. It's not going to be easy, but I know what needs to be done and how to get it done. I strongly believe that you and Dawn will not be disappointed again. Please also know in your heart that everything we implement to secure Dawn's immediate release and compensation is based on case law."

We walked out of Panera Bread floating on clouds. The words of President George Bush Sr. came to mind and felt very real. In his speech to a session of the Supreme Soviet of

Ukraine, on August 1, 1991, he said, "When Americans talk of freedom, we refer to peoples' abilities to live without fear of government intrusion, without fear of their fellow citizens, without harassment by restricting others' freedoms. We do not consider freedom a privilege to be doled out only to those who hold proper political views or belong to a certain group."

CHAPTER 19
The Joys of Activism

B onnie flew into Detroit from New York on December 23. Issa picked her up, and she stayed in the extra room in their suite. He was excited about her arrival; I was leery. She began setting up meetings with investors and wanted me to attend a meeting the day after Christmas with a Captain David, the chief of police. She called Captain David a millionaire. I was apprehensive and exhausted.

The documentary was taking a good portion of my time, keeping me up until two or three in the morning, not that my son allowed me to sleep through the night. My correspondence with Dawn and her family went on all day. We consistently informed each other of the ins and outs of what was going on. Dawn was hooked on slurping information because it helped keep her going. It became difficult to answer the prison calls that sometimes came at inappropriate times, like when I had company, was interviewing someone, or trying to walk my children in a heavy traffic parking lot to get to my car. You couldn't just pick up and say, "Can I call you later?" Once you answered the phone, you were stuck on it for fifteen minutes, time that was valuable for Dawn because she was only permitted a certain number of minutes per month. Yet I felt guilty when I didn't answer calls since I knew she'd stood in a long line to be able to make them to begin with.

The advocacy for Dawn's case was another thing that took a toll on me. I had not signed up for that role, but whenever I covered a story and met with someone from a political office or media outlet who I thought could help, I sat there for hours telling them about the case. I would follow up with an email or phone calls, on many occasions meet up again, and then I'd be introduced to another person with political muscle, and on and on. Yet nothing would transpire. Several times I decided I would not meet with anyone anymore, that I would concentrate on the story itself, but then a flicker of hope would arise when sitting across of an influential figure, and I'd be in the same boat once again.

I was relieved when Linda officially hired Issa to lead the advocacy campaign. He was better suited for it. Myself, I did not care to prosecute or disbar anyone involved in Dawn's case. That was not my style. My solutions were tribal, thus basic and simple. You just take a key, unlock Dawn's prison cell, and let her out.

"You look great," I said to Bonnie as I approached the apartment complex.

She stood at the door, looking, as always, like a model. We kissed and hugged and began chatting as if no time had lapsed between us, as if she hadn't driven me insane with her shenanigans not long ago. She squeezed my hand and led me toward the hallway to what looked like a separate apartment. "Let me show you my room," she said. "It's like a five-star hotel room."

The room was nice with bright white colors. Bonnie's luggage was in the corner, some open with clothes trailing out like pearls out of their oysters. Laughing giddily, she led me to the kitchen, where she had set up pastries on the kitchen counter. I poured myself a cup of coffee then helped move the pastries to the living room.

"Merry Christmas," Issa said, coming out of one of the rooms.

"Merry Christmas," we said.

He sat down, rubbed his jeans. "Is David on his way?" he asked Bonnie.

"Yes, he's running a little late."

"Okay, okay. No worries. Weam, how are you doing with your project?"

"I'm all right, I guess. It's just so hard with all the information that keeps pouring in. Plus, I don't have an ending yet."

"Don't worry about that, Weam. Write a great story and all else will follow. The poor girl is in there and her mother is ready to have another stroke and there are vultures around trying to nitpick at anything."

The doorbell rang and Bonnie sprung to her feet. "That's David!" She quickly glanced at me. "He's going to help Dawn, you'll see!"

"The day I watched clips of the documentary, seeing Dawn's mom cry like that, I couldn't sleep all night," David said. "I can't believe what happened in her case."

David was a handsome man in his mid to late forties. He had soft, caring eyes, and for the first time in a long time I was appreciative of Bonnie's efforts. I filled him in on some of the things I'd learned about this case. Before the trial, the government filed a motion to prevent the defendants from questioning Agent Wallace about his interviews with Emad. They also edited the statement Emad submitted to the court, leaving out the details about the project being supported by the United States government and intended to take out Saddam. During closing arguments, Prosecutor Martin said this about Emad's written testimony:

> This is the testimony that Emad would have given had he testified. The government has stipulated to this, but I want to caution you that that does not mean that the government agrees that this is the truth. We're simply agreeing that this is what he would say. You see, it was never his intention to come here and look you in the eye and tell you these things. It was never his intention to come here and answer my questions or Miss McQuade's questions. No, this was given to you from the comfort and safety of the United Kingdom. Now you may ask yourself, why isn't Emad on trial too? 'Cause he's a co-conspirator. Well, the Judge will instruct you that your

focus should be on these defendants. And the
fact that other co-conspirators aren't on trial
doesn't matter. This person is the defendants'
partner in crime, and this stipulation isn't
worth the paper it's printed on. You should
reject it.

"Have you ever heard of Vincent Bugliosi?"
Issa asked. David simply looked at Issa.

"Bugliosi is best known for prosecuting Charles Manson," Issa said. "Then he co-wrote a book about the case,
Helter Skelter, which became a bestseller. That was just the
beginning of his career. The *Los Angeles Times* called him 'An
American master of common sense.' Of felony jury trials,
this guy was successful 105 of 106 times. That's 105 of 106.
Can I show you some clips of the documentary for his film?"

Issa put in a DVD copy of *The Prosecution of George W.
Bush.*

Bonnie looked at me worriedly and whispered, "Why he
is talking about Bush? David is a Republic." That was her way
of saying Republican.

I tried to interject, but Issa was carried away like an actor
performing a Shakespeare play on stage.

"The strongest evidence against Bush is when he gave a
speech on October 7, 2002, saying that Iraq posed a threat to
the security of the United States and was capable of attacking
America at any time with his stockpile of weapons of mass
destruction. A week before that, the National Intelligence
Estimate said that Iraq did have weapons of mass destruction capabilities, but it had no plans to use it except in the

capacity of self-defense. Bugliosi says that the president and his administration edited the 'White Paper,' or the declassified version of the NIE released to Congress and the public, and censored it in a way that made the Iraqi threat seem more threatening than it actually was." He pressed play on the DVD. "You have to watch this!"

Clips of the documentary came on. We watched while eating the sweets. I wondered if Issa was trying to weasel his project into my territory.

"At what stage is Dawn's case at right now?" David asked me.

"It's under appeal," I said.

"Please, please," Issa interrupted. "These clips will only take a few minutes and they are so important!"

I excused myself to get more coffee. Bonnie followed me.

"Why is he talking about Bush?" She bit her lower lip worriedly. "David is a Republic."

"I don't know."

"I thought we were here for the Dawn story!"

"I'll try to change the subject."

We returned to the living room. Issa was on his feet, telling David more about George W. Bush's illegal activities.

"This entire project is more than just a movie, DVD, or profit," Issa said. "This whole endeavor is about informing the American people that under current laws, George W. Bush and his gang are guilty of murder and are subject to answer to the existing laws. It only takes one grand jury to indict the GW and his cabal." He looked at David pleadingly. "This project needs a mere $50,000 to be completed."

Issa tried to contact me that night, but I could not speak to him. My head hurt, and so I emailed him that I have to put the kids to bed, was tired, and it would just have to wait until tomorrow. I called Linda, but she did not answer. The following morning, Linda apologized for missing my call. "I took a sleeping pill and went to bed very early," she wrote, "to lock out the worries for a while."

I decided not to let her in on what had taken place the night before.

"How did your meeting go last night?" she asked once we were on the phone.

"It was okay. I'll tell you about it later."

"You know when Darrin met with Issa the other day, he was really impressed. He said, this guy gets it, he's like, one, two, three. Dawn thinks the same of him. She thinks he's very professional, and well, normal, like us."

I wanted to get off the phone as quickly as possible.

"Did he tell you if he contacted anyone so far? He said it would take him about four weeks to get it all done and that he would send me daily updates, but he hasn't done that yet. Dawn called me earlier. She's wondering about that too."

"Linda, let me talk to you later," I said.

I sat in my chair and stared out the window at the evergreens. The snow weighed the tree branches down like a large hat over a load of curly hair. No squirrels or birds were around this morning. It was that cold. I remembered the freezing temperatures Dawn had written to me about. The prison's heater had broken, and it was so cold that the milk on Dawn's windowsill froze. There was a million dollar repair needed to fix the leak in the facility's boiler. Dawn was freezing even though she had on four shirts and two pairs of socks. The extra blankets were taken away a month prior, so the inmates had only one blanket. Anyone who was caught with more than one blanket got an incident report. One of the guards, Mr. Cox, said it was so cold on the third floor he felt sorry for the women when counting. Most people hung out near the heaters that did work and others just said fuck it, they would take an incident report for having more than one blanket because they were afraid of getting pneumonia.

I went to the kitchen and poured a fresh cup of coffee, leaned over the countertop, and dialed Issa's number. I hoped that whatever happened yesterday was a mistake or a misunderstanding and that he would follow through with his promise to help Dawn.

"Weam, I believe you're a sincere person and that you would do anything to help," he said, and mentioned three or four things to prove his point. "But Bonnie is nuts! I can work with anyone, but she is not normal! She has issues. Serious issues. Honestly, I question your judgment."

"What? I told you…"

"Can you let me finish?"

I was quiet.

"We were in a restaurant, and she said she was going to introduce us to Princess Ranya. I thought, wow, this woman is brilliant! She brought over the Princess of Jordan. Turns out the woman Bonnie introduced us to *thought* she was the princess of Dearborn!"

It took a lot of effort not to laugh.

"Bonnie believes in a lot of things that are not real. If after a year of knowing her you didn't realize the severity of the damage she does, I'm puzzled. You arbitrarily decided to bring on Bonnie..."

"Issa, I told you Bonnie is crazy, but you are using her craziness to distract from what happened yesterday when you had me sit in a three-hour meeting listening to something that did not pertain to why I came in the first place."

"I thought you are someone I can communicate with," he said, exasperated. "You don't understand the situation you threw me in with that Bonnie. Not only that, but I have to accommodate her entourage. She has demoralized us. She comes in at ten at night and she runs off without telling us where she's going. We don't know the meeting happens until it happens. Honestly, I question your judgment!"

"Stop changing the subject. You tried to steal the investor yesterday!"

"Is that what you think? Weam, I talked to Bonnie before David came over and we agreed that we'd approach him about the Bugliosi story."

"Oh, and did you also decide not to fill me in on that?"

"You came very late—"

"We talked quite a bit—"

"I forgot, okay? I was busy wanting to learn a couple of more things about Dawn's case before I met with her mother today. I've been barking all along and I'm disappointed. When I speak, people of intellect listen with earnest. Salem and I cuss each other out, but we have roots. We're true to the cause."

"I'm true to my cause too, which you were hired to work on. Yet you haven't sent Linda or Dawn any updates like you told them you would."

"I told you that Dawn was a victim and the prosecutors are guilty of misconduct and should be indicted and convicted. We have the upper advantage. We will get the girl out. We're going to deliver. If they don't like how I do it, too bad. I'm going to get this done. I've got this whole thing laid out. We just need a little cash and some volunteers. Tell Dawn to relax and not to piss me off. You guys have had a year and a half on this and it's Christmas. I haven't been able to do much. Give me a break! I'm the only one who can get her out. But first, I can't have Bonnie stay here another minute! I want her out now!"

That afternoon, Salem delivered Bonnie to my door. She sauntered into my home, the sound of her heels loud against my kitchen tile. The fragrance of perfume and makeup distributed to whichever area she stepped into, like when a priest spreads incense during mass. She greeted the children with utmost sweetness, like a flower. She called my son "my fiancé" and my daughter "sunshine." Her mannerism and the innocence in her face diluted any anger one might have against her.

Salem went to get her luggage. A moment later, he returned with his head bowed in embarrassment. Salem reminded me of the gallant men in the olden days. He was quiet, shy, and reserved, and he wouldn't look a woman in the eyes. He was so respectful. You could entrust him with a flower petal and it would be returned without a single crease.

We sat at the kitchen table. I served them cardamom tea and *keleicha*, traditional Iraqi cookies, along with sesame puree and date syrup. Bonnie asked if she could hold my son, who was resting against my hip. I told her I was used to working like that.

"Even if you put a knife against my throat, I will never again deal with Issa." Bonnie dove into the subject. She then took a bite of the *keleicha* and complimented me on them.

"I did not make them," I said. "My in-laws did."

"Hmmm, they are very tasty."

Salem and I looked at each other. The phone rang. It was Issa.

"Weam, why did you initiate one mistake into a series of monumental mistakes?"

"Issa, I can't talk right now. Do you need something important?"

"Tell Bonnie that she can come back, but just to keep focused on her work," he said, returned to his calm self. "I'm not the type of man who would throw someone out on the streets, a woman on top of that."

"She's not on the streets, and I will tell her."

I hung up the phone, placed my son on the living room floor, and sat at the table.

Salem smiled kindly. "This has been blown way out of proportion."

"I swear, on my life…"

"Hold on Bonnie," I said, then turned to Salem. "I agree with you. But Issa can't go off like that. He feels guilty about what he did yesterday, and to make himself feel better, he's putting the whole blame on us."

"I don't know about that thing yesterday," Salem said. "But Issa is under a lot of stress. He has run out of resources and put himself in a bad spot. He lost his family even, and he's pretty much out to dry."

I lowered my eyes. I could sympathize with depleting yourself for a project you believe in which has valuable information and costs pennies in comparison to the thousands of horror and action films easily being made. I looked at Bonnie. "Will you go back to Issa's house?"

"Only if the Virgin Mary came down right now and asked me to," she said. "Otherwise, no!"

The Virgin Mary did not come right then, which meant Bonnie was staying at my house that night.

CHAPTER 20
Visiting Dawn in Prison

Darrin was flying me and Dawn's sister-in-law, Kristin, to the prison to visit Dawn. Kristin sat in the back of the four-seat plane. We were going 150 miles per hour and headed straight into the clouds. Once the air cleared, the Ohio River appeared. From 8000 feet high, it looked like a cobra flexing its scale into the shape of an "S." The airplane was encrusted by more clouds, and then the flight got bumpy. I looked at our pilot with a worrisome expression.

Darrin laughed. "It's just a little turbulence," he said through the intercom system that allowed everyone on board to communicate. We were all wearing noise-reducing headsets.

"But it's a beautiful day outside," I said.

"Turbulence is not only due to weather conditions," he said.

"What would happen if a flock of birds hit the window?"

I asked.

"The likeliness of a bird hitting the window is like your car stalling on a train track. Birds and planes are like cars and people. You don't hit each other. When you fly toward a bird, they fly away. Of course, there are some mentally ill birds…"

"What if an eagle hits the window?" I asked.

He laughed. "Maybe if a pterodactyl hits it, then we would be in trouble."

I was quiet.

"A pterodactyl is a large dinosaur that can fly."

"How did you know I didn't know what the word meant?"

"I could tell by your reaction."

A call from Air Traffic Control came in and Darrin talked to them. I gazed out the window and thought about Dawn. I was excited to finally meet her in person. For the past six months, we had talked on the phone and emailed one another endlessly, but had it not been for pictures, we would not know what the other looked like. Linda had wanted me to visit Dawn from the start, but as long as we were driving there, that was out of the question. The drive was approximately seven hours, depending on construction.

The first year of visiting Dawn in prison, the Hanna's itinerary went something like this: They left their house at five o'clock the night before, on a Saturday, and got to Lexington, Kentucky at around midnight. At 12:30 am, they stopped for a quick dinner. Then they rented a hotel room. Because they were regulars and they were family visiting family, the owner of the Blue Grass Inn gave them a deal of $75 a night. They all crammed into one hotel room and then woke up early the next morning to visit Dawn at nine. Visiting hours ended at three in the afternoon, during which time the family headed out. Without stopping, they got home at about ten at night. They picked up a pizza on the way and ate it in the car since it was already late Sunday night and the next day they had to go to work.

Then Darrin got his pilot's license in December 2010 and started flying to Kentucky. The flight was approximately two and a half hours each way, so it was more doable for me to leave my kids for only one day. Right after the holidays, during the first week of January, Linda received an email from Deday LaRene informing her that the Sixth Circuit Court had set Dawn's appeal for oral argument to March 11. This information created a new frenzy of hope, so I quickly went back to working on the documentary. We had not gotten the funding that we needed, but we had enough to pay the editor and do Part I, which told enough of the story to create the support we were looking for and to play the film at the Arab American National Museum.

"What ever happened with Issa?" Darrin asked me. "He seemed really enthusiastic about this case and confident that he could create a positive outcome."

"Everyone who hears about this case thinks they can be the hero who will rescue Dawn and make a difference in the world."

I looked out the window and watched the scenery beneath me, the green pastures, the highways and cars, and the horse ranches that decorated the earth with an abundance of color, like an Indian bride. I didn't want to say too much since Darrin did not know that Linda had hired Issa to play advocate. After his fallout with me and Bonnie, I never heard

from Issa again and I did not want to contact him. Bonnie did a little disappearing act as well. Issa offered to return Linda her money, minus expenses, but then he stopped taking her calls. We assumed that he had already spent the money and had nothing to pay back. Over a cup of coffee, we went over his enthusiastic words, like, "We need to bombard the prosecutor with 400 to 500 emails and that's just saying 'hello.' We must tell her, 'Do your job or we will get somebody else who will.'" When Linda had told Issa that Ron Scott had met with the prosecutor, he said, "He should have never approached the prosecutor because now she's no longer afraid."

Yeah, he was a real cowboy.

Linda felt stuck. Dawn raged about Issa taking off the way he did, swore that she would sue his ass once she was out of prison. She would go to LA herself if she had to. Linda worried that if Darrin found out, he would get upset at her for allowing yet another person to take advantage of her desperate need to get her daughter out of prison. Feeling guilty to have introduced the Hannas to Issa, I came up with the idea of writing a letter to Bugliosi in the hopes that he would pressure Issa to return the money and, more importantly, as a top-notch attorney, he would help Dawn somehow.

One day my phone rang, and seeing the "Unknown Caller" ID, I assumed it was Dawn. It was actually Vincent Bugliosi wanting to learn the details of what had transpired between Issa and the Hanna family. I locked myself in one of the house rooms and explained to Mr. Bugliosi what happened. He asked quick questions. I answered. It dawned on me during the questioning that I was talking to one of the greatest US prosecutors. I got a little nervous, but that went away when I thought of Issa's passion for justice and the predicament he was in now. "Mr. Bugliosi, Issa is not a bad guy."

"He's not?"

"No. It was not his intention to hurt anyone. He was desperate. He had put everything he had into the convicting Bush project. It's my understanding that his personal life was hugely affected by this. I think he's not returning the money because he doesn't have it."

"So he was in a bind that he didn't know how to get out of?"

"Yes. He really believes in your project, as I do. I appreciate what you're doing. In your book, you addressed a lot of issues that the Iraqi American community has brought up, but no one wants to listen. Your work is based not only on facts, but sensible feelings. Those pictures you have of Bush laughing like he's at a party when there's a war going on and people are dying says it all. He was in euphoria 99.99 percent of the time. A lot of Americans died in this war, senselessly. And even more Iraqis!"

"I don't forget the over 100,000 innocent Iraqi men, women, and even babies who have died horrible, violent deaths."

"That's why Dawn's case is so relevant to me," I said. "She is nothing but a distraction from the real crimes taking place that no one is held accountable for."

Before he hung up, Bugliosi promised that until his dying day, he would make sure that George W. Bush paid for the crimes he'd committed.

"Thank you," I said, feeling incredibly foolish that I'd taken up this important man's time with such a frivolous matter when he worked seven days a week, from 10 am to 2 am, and in seven years, he had taken only three days off to celebrate his fiftieth wedding anniversary. I also felt sad for Issa. The film industry said a lot about peoples' standards of living. The truth was that the general public preferred junk over healthfulness. Whether it related to food for the body, mind, or soul, it made no difference. My brother once owned a video store, and he was amazed at his customers when they eagerly reserved and rented *Friday the 13th* instead of *Gandhi*.

Bugliosi passed away in June 2015, at the age of 80.

The moment we landed, I called Linda to check on the kids. She had offered to watch them. Linda was the first person outside of family who had babysat my children. I trusted this nurturing woman whose desire was to one day lead a quiet life on a farm; who regularly filled a five-gallon bucket with apples, carrots, sweet beets, corn or whatever else she had on hand and left it out at night for the visiting bunnies, squirrels, and deer, one of which was pregnant; who would surprise us with an early morning invitation on a cold snowy day to pack up the kids in their pajamas for a breakfast of pancakes or a cookie-making extravaganza; who, on Christmas, carried through my front door a huge triceratops named Kota, along with a pamphlet that explained how to maintain and feed this "interactive animatronic dinosaur" – his food was a plastic leaf so huge it looked like a hand fan. My children rode Kota like a horse.

I had really wanted Linda to visit Dawn with us, but Darrin was against the idea. He was afraid she would have another stroke. "Dawn is like someone on a raft, way out there in the middle of a large ocean," he said. "When they see someone, they grab them. The person that saves the drowning person sinks, and now you have two people dead."

It wasn't only Darrin who did not want her to go. Linda did not want to go either. "It's very, very hard leaving my daughter there," she told me.

The Federal Medical Center (FMY) in Lexington, Kentucky is an administrative facility for male inmates. The facility adjacent to it is a minimum security satellite camp for female inmates. The prison was once called The Narcotic Farm and was notorious for allegedly treating and punishing addicts. Apparently, most people arrested for drugs were sent there between 1935 and 1975. In an article published October 24, 2008, by *Scientific American*, Charles Q. Choi wrote that there is a documentary that chronicles how the Farm was shut down just as Congress discovered that researchers there were using patients as human guinea pigs in CIA-funded experiments with LSD.

The following day, *Scientific American* released the following correction:

> When originally posted, this story suggested that a Congressional investigation into the Narcotic Farm had led to its closure. In fact the main reason Narco was closed was that its centralized form of institutional care was supplanted by a national network of local treatment centers. Its closure coincided with

the Congressional investigation into LSD
research. Scientific American regrets the
error.

The women's prison looked like an old fashioned British
dormitory school with green grass in the front and a nice
sized parking lot. There was a big yard where the women
could play sports or walk to the end of the yard and back –
back and forth, back and forth, and back and forth. There
were a few picnic tables near the visitor's entrance. If you
sat there, you could sometimes see the men next door play
outside.

As we went down the stairs that led to the main entrance,
a side door opened. Dawn and an elderly black woman
laughed and waved at us. The sight of them startled me, but
Darrin and Kristin were not surprised. "What kind of prison
is this?" I asked. "They could just walk off without anyone
knowing."

"It's low security," Darrin said, "since no one here is in
for violent crimes."

"No wonder Dawn is always threatening to run away. It
would be so easy if she did."

The visiting room was one open space area with a
security guard, a few kids' toys, and vending machines
which Linda already forewarned me did not have coffee. We
each filled out a paper and grabbed a table as we waited for
Dawn to come out. I wondered if any of the inmates in the
visiting room were the ones that Dawn wrote to me about,
the ones who called her a fucking Arab and terrorist or who
"accidentally" spilled hot coffee on her arm or pressed a hot

skillet against her.

The inmates, with their green uniforms, were either black women or had blonde hair and light complexion, so I knew none could be the two Chaldean sisters who were serving time for food stamp fraud. The sisters were also regularly picked on and called "the Twin Towers." Their two brothers were sent to jail too for this food stamp fraud. The four siblings had the same judge that sentenced Dawn. They had begged and begged the Judge to let at least one of them stay home to care for the parents, who were in their seventies and eighties, and when one was done with the prison sentence, allow the other to go. The Judge refused. Not even sixty-five days after the siblings were in prison, their mother had a heart attack and died.

"I would love to see Lisa here," I said, looking around.

"Yeah, Lisa is a character," Darrin said.

Lisa was the seventy-six year old "Jewish Princess" Dawn often told me about. Like Dawn, inmates hated her because she had money, tapping her commissary limit every month and buying yarn weekly. The last time the prison had pork chop night, Lisa went to everyone and said, "Do you eat pork? Can I have your pork chops?"

"She's so Jewish, but you gotta love her," Dawn wrote to me. "People make fun of us because if I need anything I go to her and vice versa. Between the Arab and Jew, they say, we have everything. It's true. I'm always running out of mayonnaise and she always needs brown rice so it works out well. Once in a while, she asks me for ice cream. I can't deny a seventy-six-year-old woman ice cream. She's someone's mother and grandmother, so yes, what flavor do you want is what always comes out of my mouth. She looks so happy and almost always selects Butter Nut Crunch."

Lisa was known to make smart ass comments to everyone and one day really pissed off Dawn. A girl put two donuts on Dawn's tray for lunch, and Dawn had to pass Lisa to go through the cafeteria because Lisa's job was wiping tables. When Lisa saw Dawn, she said, "Oh, hi, slim!" and looked at the donuts.

Dawn finally appeared, glowing with excitement. The energy in the room changed. I stopped observing and feeling sorry for the inmates around me and got up to hug and kiss Dawn.

"You look like an Arab," she said as she sat down.

"So do you," I said.

"I'm starving! Darrin, can you get me some food from the vending machine?" She returned her attention to me. "I think most all Chaldeans are related, aren't they? I don't really know how this works, but it's a strange dynamic. I once dated a guy, then found out he was like a third cousin. Kind of gross."

"My husband and I are related," I said.

"That's way too close for comfort. It's weird, kind of like a hillbilly. Your aunt actually becomes your mother-in-law. It's like Billy Joe Jim Bob, with a liquor store and money. So whaddaya say, cuz? Wanna work together? No, better yet." She tapped my shoulder, which was moving up and down from laughter. "We are related. Can I borrow $25,000, never pay you back, and then add a twist to the story when family gets involved. Isn't that how it's done?"

Darrin returned and laid in front of her all sorts of junk food.

"Have you heard anything?" she asked, eagerly opening the bags of chips, candy, and cakes.

Darrin told her what had happened during the oral arguments, per his conversation with Deday. They talked about the three judges. One was a long time progressive icon, the other two were Bush II appointees. Deday said, "Our hope mostly lies with Damon Jerome Keith." The progressive icon.

"I asked Deday what kind of questions the judges asked at the oral argument," Dawn said. "Did anything come up about the Brady Violation? Civil rights? Hiding evidence? Ex parte anything? The evidentiary hearing? He said, 'As I told you before, it is unwise to jump to conclusions based on the things said by judges at oral argument.' I was like, whatever!"

She finished one chocolate bar and began on another one.

"Then he says something like, 'The two Bush II appointees asked some very good questions and it was overall a livelier than usual session, which is good. One judge asked about whether the CIA evidence might mislead the jury into acquitting because *'it just isn't right'* to prosecute under the circumstances. Deday answered them, 'the government could have asked for a limiting instruction.'"

She gulped down a soda.

"I asked Deday if Judge Keith was awake. He's, like, eighty-nine? He said, 'He was definitely awake and grinning appropriately from time to time to my extremely witty remarks. Like myself, he's old, not dead.' I asked Deday what was the question Keith smiled at, and he answered, 'The one about the goat.'"

We laughed.

"His answer is stupid." She turned to Darrin and asked for more junk food.

We talked about her uncle Najib Shemami, the spy. A few days after Dawn's oral argument, the *Detroit Free Press* published an article about Najib that was titled "Cancer-ridden Iraqi spy must report to N.C. prison, judge rules." Shemami, 61, had to report to a federal prison in North Carolina by Friday, March 18 to begin his forty-six-month sentence, which had been delayed nine times.

"I read his indictment and his sentencing transcript, and it actually makes me laugh," Dawn said. "The prosecutor got him to plead guilty to a few things, like he was in Turkey, and reported that a building he saw was something that had to do with America and some top secret thing they were doing. Yeah, right! He was probably eating pistachios in a cab and looked up and saw a high rise newer looking building and asked the cab driver, 'What is that?' and the cab driver probably told him, 'Big, big, American, for American to come, big, big. Millions.'

"Najib also reported about a military hospital on a ship in the sea. I'm sure, again, he passed by the seaside in a cab in Turkey on his way to the airport and said, 'What's that big boat?' Only again to get the reply from the cab driver, 'America, America, big ship, for the oil, they will come, America, to war, make a big, big hospital in the water.' I mean, he probably went on to Iraq, and since he wanted to keep his little job of bringing shit over there, like pillow cases of clothes, hygiene stuff, and gifts, just fed them this. It kept him afloat over there, kept him an integral part of the government so no one would bother him."

Well, spying came in all forms, shapes, sizes, and weirdness. In the 1960s, the CIA spent five years and some $20 million training spy cats by implanting a clandestine listening device inside them to target the Soviet embassy. On its first field test, the spy cat was hit by a taxicab and the operation, called Operation Acoustic Kitty, was abandoned shortly thereafter. Operation Pigeon was when during World War II, a famed behavioral psychologist B.F. Skinner was enlisted by the government to try and train pigeons for use in a missile guidance system.

"I was so close to having Najib chaperone me to Iraq," I said. "But I ended up going with Raad instead." I recounted our little trip. They laughed wholeheartedly at the part where Raad dropped a large Coca-Cola cup of jalapeno peppers in the airplane aisles and then took off and hid in his seat.

"Oh, that Uncle Raad!" Dawn said. "He's such a lowlife, sorry. I put him at like 80 percent in terms of credibility but 10 percent inasmuch as class, style, manners. I once visited him at his house in Oak Park on Scotia Street, where, like, three Shemamis lived eight to ten houses apart. My cousin took me over there, and there was Raad. I call him Rod, like the fishing Rod."

She rolled her curls around her ears. "Anyway, he was sitting on the floor of a dirty carpeted living room, watching baseball or some sport, eating an entire chicken carcass with his bare hands. He pulled up the chicken, half eaten, and a leg slipped off and he said, 'Hi, Donna. Eat too, eat too.' Um... yeah, not so much. I said, 'No, no, thank you, Uncle Rod. I'm

full, I've just eaten.' I pretended I'd eaten in my car. He wanted a big giant kiss and a hug...uhm....yeah, no thanks. I said,
no, no, no, don't get up. I bent down to give him the make-
shift hug. He wouldn't let go of the chicken carcass, the whole
entire fucking chicken, most disgusting thing I've ever seen."

A young inmate walked past us and Dawn waved hello.

"She's going to take our picture in a little bit," she said.
She looked at me. "Why aren't you eating anything?"

"Your mom packed us a lunch. We ate it in the plane."
I smiled. "Linda is so cute. She sent with me a Ziploc bag of
change that weighs more than a pound to buy food from the
vending machine. I said, what, they serve steak in there? All
I need is coffee. She said, coffee is one thing they don't have."

"Yeah, sorry. No coffee."

"Don't worry about it. Continue with your story."

"So anyway, Uncle Rod's kids peeped out from the kitch-
en area and my cousin led me to the kitchen. The kitchen was
in absolute shambles. I quickly noticed the white tile floor.
It was stained red. Note to self. So, when we left, I asked my
cousin, 'Hey, why is the floor red?' She laughed and said, 'His
wife did that when she found out uncle Rod was cheating on
her. So she was either making red Jell-O or took a huge bowl
of red Jell-O and then dumped it all over the white kitch-
en floor. You could see some of it hit the white cabinets and
it stained like nothing you have ever seen. So hence, Arab
woman's reaction to husband cheating.'"

I was laughing so hard, I couldn't breathe.

"Uncle Rod. Yeah, what a prize. He's a decent uncle, he
means well. Hence, offering up his chicken carcass to me
when I walked in. He was stuffing his face with chicken like

it was the last frigging supper. He had a pile of yellow rice with raisins in it and was drinking from a two-liter."

"That chicken carcass really got to you, didn't it?" Darrin asked.

"It was kind of gross, but hey, whatever works for you." She shrugged. "The last memory I have of him was seeing him at a wedding. He was toothless or had one or two teeth, his hair thinning and gray. He looked awful, and we didn't recognize each other. Someone introduced him to me and we were like, holy shit, we are related! I had gained like a hundred pounds and he wasn't aging well."

Darrin and I were literally sliding off our chair with laughter. Kristin was laughing too, but she was much calmer about it.

"It was a sight! He seriously had to question like two or three of my cousins as to who I was. I began to recognize him by his voice and his nose. And he had a clearly recognizable odor to him, something between a bottle of beer and a Winston cigarette. But anyway, he's an okay guy."

A lot of what Dawn said she'd already written to me about it in emails. But the way she ate and spoke about it at that moment reminded me of what her mother often said. "Dawn is not the same person she was before she went into prison, and she never will be."

Dawn also reminded me of someone gasping for air, like an image I'd once seen on a YouTube video where a masked man shouted, "Allah Akbar," as he slaughtered a man by the throat, as if butchering a lamb. They were outside in the desert. The victim's body leaned to the side, and the victim made a gnawing screech as he took his last breaths. It was like Dawn had quickly inhaled what little air she had to store it for when she returned to the airless room. Her lifestyle resembled that of an ants' kingdom. Ants enslave other ants, keeping them captive and making them do work for the colony. This idea probably bit me because of "Bunkie," a woman Dawn told me about. Her real name is Theresa.

Theresa was in prison for a conspiracy to get high. She worked all of her life at a cotton mill as a threader and beamer. She can tell you how the entire cotton industry works and how blue jeans are made. From time to time, she liked to get high on the weekends with marijuana or a little meth. One day she and her boyfriend, David, were at this guy's house, Chuck, waiting to buy meth when the police busted in and then indicted all of them. Chuck ended up giving the Feds the names "David and Theresa."

"It's more like 'David,' not 'David and Theresa,'" she told Dawn, but the more names Chuck gave, the better for him.

The Feds told her she would go to prison for a long, long time if she didn't give names of people buying, cooking, or using meth. She said she couldn't help them. She only knew of one guy cooking a little meth in his trailer kitchen in North Carolina but she thought, why should she bring him down? So she took her six-years, eight-month sentence.

In her first year of prison, her son, who was in his late twenties, couldn't take his mother being gone and what happened to her. He left a note, drank anti-freeze, and killed himself. She never got to say goodbye to him, wasn't allowed to go to his funeral, and couldn't deal with his untimely death. So they immediately put her on some intense psych meds, which causes her to sleep seventeen hours a day. She says she is sleeping her time away. Most days she doesn't really know where she is.

Theresa works in the outside warehouse and she says that, without the work camps, the main prisons wouldn't operate because the government would not be able to have all these extra employees employed and pay them twelve cents per hour to handle the hard labor and get the orders, food, and supplies ready, organized, palletized, invoiced, and inventoried to send to the FCI prison.

"This is legalized slavery," Theresa said about the prison system. "You have all these people who get rounded up, all for non-violent crimes, and get put in these work camps, making twelve cents per hour."

Theresa hopes that the day will soon come that she can be off all the medications that the government put her on. She feels she is now a drug addict in prison.

"Dawn, you know what, I've never considered myself an addict. I was a tax payin', law abidin', good citizen from North Carolina and that didn't pay off. The Feds killed my son, gave my boyfriend ten years for being interested in the meth recipe which he never cooked, and they made me a drug addict in prison. I have to go to the pill line twice a day to get my pills and they are in such a high dosage, I can't function without them."

When it was time to leave, the energy in the room changed again. The reality that Dawn described in her letters of what took place inside the prison set in. Her stories trickled through my mind, one by one, like drops of medicine. There were the lesbianism stories, which she and her friends referred to as the PLCs (Pussy Licking Club/Contest) because, she wrote, "The way in which these nasty bitches just lick on each other and trade on and off, you can hardly keep up. The women don't even frickin' know each other, and they switch up all the time. Crystal with Jessica, then Jessica with Sasha, then Laverne with Crystal, then Laverne with Michelle. It's truly a contest."

With one couple, the stud in the relationship abused the other woman. Both women were married with children, and the abused woman told Dawn that she was not proud of herself and struggled to fight her sexual urges. Dawn wrote, "Her girlfriend is so aggressive, it's terrible. She put her up against the wall and said, 'You will be with me when I'm in da house! It is what it is!' The best is when one got mad when the other went on a visit with her husband and four kids who came to see her. The rest of the week, they were fighting. Thank God the abused woman leaves in a few months." On a brighter note, on Sweetest Day, one couple did a candlelight dinner up on the third floor with stolen food from the kitchen and a make-believe limo service to pick up the couple. They did get in trouble, though.

We cleared the table of all candy wrappers and chip bags. We posed for "professional" pictures, and then Dawn walked us to the security guard. "All the girls drool over him," she said.

The guard was nice and handsome. He had a tattoo in Arabic on his upper arm. I forgot what it said, but I asked him where he got it.

"I served in Iraq," he said.

"An Iraqi did the tattoo?"

"Yes."

"How did you know what he was writing on there?"

He laughed. "I showed it to the interpreter who worked with us."

"Oh, smart idea!"

He laughed. I hugged Dawn goodbye.

"The next time I see you will be at your mother's house," I said.

She bowed her head. "Yeah."

"Or you will come over for dinner. Eat my dolma and barbecue."

She nodded. She didn't seem convinced.

Darrin and I walked out. The temperature had dropped. It felt cold and sad. We were quiet until halfway through our drive.

"When we leave, she seems all right, she seems in pretty good spirits," Darrin said. "But I don't really know how she feels when she goes back in. I know that she's always very hopeful that very soon, we're on the verge of someone actually correcting this problem and saying, 'Hey, wait, this is wrong, let's fix it.'"

I watched him make numerous calls and talk to several people about his sister's case.

"You have a lot on your plate," I said.

"I always tell people I have three jobs," he said. "I teach at the university, I work with the mental health automation system, and my third job is this – trying to get justice for Dawn."

He filed a flight plan over his phone. "We've got to get back because there's, like, two thunderstorms and there's this gap in-between that's just rain. We need to go to that gap. Air traffic control will be watching us so it's not like we're accidentally going to be, you know…"

"Oh, okay," I interrupted, happy that we were going to watch the movie *Mamma Mia!* during the flight back.

CHAPTER 21
Which Department to Call for Justice

As the tenth anniversary of September 11 neared, NAAJA (National Arab American Journalists Association) held its sixth annual conference titled "Strengthening the Voices of American Arabs." Its objectives were to address challenges journalists faced in the pro-Democracy movement in the Middle East and Arab world. The conference was from Friday, April 29 to Sunday, May 1 at the Hyatt Regency in Dearborn, Michigan. Saturday's schedule featured ten panel discussions, one of which I was a speaker at, in Room B, from 9 to 10:10 am. My session was called "The Telling of our Stories through Online and Video Media Methods."

After I signed in and received my name tag, I grabbed a coffee and a program booklet on the way to Room B. I skimmed through the pages and noticed that following my panel, in the same room, four speakers were going to talk about "Civil Rights and American Arabs: 10 years after 9/11."

I knew two of these speakers, Ron Scott and Imad Hamad. They had been advocating for Dawn's release since the very beginning. I wanted to meet the third one – Dawud Walid, the Executive Director of the Council on American-Islamic Relations (CAIR), Michigan branch. A number of people suggested bringing CAIR, a very powerful organization, on board to help with Dawn's cause, especially since Amnesty and the ACLU said they could not get involved.

The speakers took their seats, except for Ron Scott. He was nowhere in sight. Dawud Walid went up to the podium. He was a well-built African American man with a round face and a stubble beard and moustache. He had on a black suit and a dark red checkered tie.

"We complain about how the media views Arab Americans," he said, "but until Arab Americans get involved in journalism, become those people who are over the editorial staff, we're going to keep getting the same of what we've been getting." Lightly tapping his fingertips on the podium, he continued. "The Jewish experience is very rich, and we should draw from it. Jewish Americans were involved in the civil rights movements. I challenge our community in that we need to stand up and get involved in other peoples' struggles as well, and this will help bring us more friends to support us."

Imad Hamad went to the podium next. At the time, Imad was Michigan's regional director of the American Arab Discrimination Committee, otherwise known as ADC, founded in 1980. Imad is a short man who normally wears a black cowboy hat. He spoke with no pauses and there were no periods at the end of his sentences, so I didn't try to take notes as I normally liked to do. Instead I half listened to his lecture, half remembered the day our film crew went to his office in Dearborn. His office walls were filled with stuff: the American flag; awards; pictures of President Obama and other political figures he'd stood with while wearing his black cowboy hat.

Imad had met with ADC's national office and the Chaldean Federation of America and initiated joint efforts with the local US attorney office in the eastern district, appealing for the government to be fair and transparent in dealing with Dawn's case. They requested that the US Department of Justice, the civil rights division in DC, review the case.

"I know many people who did business in Iraq that didn't face what Dawn faced," Imad said at his office, addressing Dawn's father and her brothers. "Since the national tragedy of 9/11, things changed. There is a new reality, a new political climate. People are intimidated by the fear factor and retaliation and this has added to people not trusting the government. That's why the whole nation has been debating civil rights and liberties versus safety and national security, like they go against each other. Since the foundation of this great nation, they complemented each other."

"The thing is, we have no crime," Darrin had said to Imad. "We have no criminal. There's no equipment that got where it shouldn't have. This was a USA operation."

"When it comes to Iraq, it becomes more of a political flavor case rather than judicial."

"We're talking here about people's lives!" Darrin said, frustrated. "Is there anything else that we can do to get to Holder? He's supposed to be totally against this type of, as you say, politically flavored cases."

"I really can understand your frustration and concerns. I deal with these cases maybe on a daily basis. Unfortunately, as of September 11, as I said, the rules of engagement with the government about this are limited to certain channels. Now we don't want to be perceived to be accepting political pressure. They heard it, and they heard it loud and clear in Dawn's case."

"When they heard it from you, *loud and clear*, they still put her in prison."

"I understand, but my friend, that's not going to stop the proceedings. At the end of the day, keep in mind one thing. When the government launches a so-called investigation for a number of years, invest a great deal of resources, and then put the allegations against an individual, it becomes a must for that government to save face and prove their case."

"But is this good enough, this, 'Well, we'll just keep going with the system.' This is her life. There's only one person here that suffers and that's Dawn. The people of America have absolutely no reason to have her in prison. I think they'd want her out. All the government keeps doing is trying to win, keep trying to win." Darrin shrugged. "I don't know... what are they telling you? Are they telling you what you want to hear to make you feel good?"

"The system is heartless," Imad said with a grin, as if finally cutting to the chase. "The only difference between us versus them, between people and government, if you want to put it in that category, is that the government is heartless. Period. Maybe to a prosecutor, to a case worker, an agent, a person is nothing but a file. A case. A paper. Information.

What's in ink."

"If Arab Americans are being persecuted, and like you said, there's many more cases like Dawn's, is our best response as a community is just to say, 'We'll write a letter. We don't like it. We'll argue with you. We'll even bring it to national attention, and we understand that it's just a file to you. We understand it's going to take time and the people are going to be persecuted and that's it.' Is that the best we can do?"

"No. But, I think, my friend, we will not do ourselves a great service if we don't realize the reality as is. We're dealing with a great deal of challenges. This will be a bitter, long fight, and the record is not going to get set straight without victims and many injustices as a cost. Dawn's situation, like many other situations, will serve as a reminder to all of us in this country to ask, 'Where are we going?'"

"But instead of asking the government to fix it and pushing them to fix it...it sounds like we're just saying to..."

"No, no, no, no, no. Now, I think we have one of the greatest systems. That doesn't make it perfect. The government is not god and cannot be god. No one owns the truth. It's not fair to underestimate the importance of our work as people. Without it, we'd submit to a police state and no longer be America. Justice is our true American value. Even the government cannot take that away from us as citizens. American fairness cannot be compromised."

* * *

The session on civil rights was over, and as the majority of people walked out of the room, I approached Dawud Walid to introduce myself. I told him I was doing a documentary about the Dawn Hanna case.

"I've heard about the Dawn Hanna case," he said.

"Ron Scott and Imad Hamad have been strong advocates for Dawn."

"I know. Ron Scott is a very good friend of mine. And Imad Hamad and I have worked on a number of cases together."

"Some suggested that CAIR could help Dawn as well, that the more organizations worked on behalf of her case, the stronger it would be. I was wondering if you'd be willing to meet with the Hanna family sometime next week."

"Yes, I would like that."

We exchanged business cards and I walked outside. I saw Ron Scott sitting at a table in the hallway. I walked up to him.

"I was looking for you in there," I said. "Your name was on the program booklet."

He shook his head regretfully. "They didn't call me to remind me about the conference."

"They sent many email reminders. Didn't you get them?"

"Well, I don't use email very much."

I smiled, remembering what Linda said about me wanting to send him an email. "Don't bother. He won't check it."

Ron Scott, an African American man, was tall and had white hair. He carried himself in a dignified and calm manner. He had a deep voice, but he was soft-spoken.

"Do you think the judges will release Dawn?" I asked him. Her appeal for oral argument was March 11 and everyone was simply waiting for the verdict. "I have a lot of hope that they will, but Linda and her family have no faith left in the judicial system."

He bowed his head lightly and flipped through the edges of the papers in his hands. "What they did is illegal," he said. He looked at me and smiled. "It's illegal."

There was a moment of silence.

"An all-American girl from Rochester Hills was set up – essentially, I just say it the way it is - and locked up and it could be any one of us."

"What disturbs me is that the Hannas were once a patriotic family who had the American flag flying outside their home." I remembered the *Justice for Dawn* banner that stood on Linda's front lawn, in place of the flag. It was once new and sturdy, but as time went by, the banner began to fall apart. These days the banner is held up by one rod as the remainder of it twirls over the grass like a dress over a bed post. "Now they are not so patriotic," I said.

He smiled knowingly. "Oh, but they still are, even more than before. Through this experience, and their efforts and their story, they are serving the United States, regardless of how they look at it."

"There's nothing that can be done?"

He slowly leaned back in his seat. "There's not a day that we're not working on the case. But like I said before, it's like pulling alligator teeth." He sighed. "Her case exhibits just how challenging it is at this particular time for the American people to deal with their government. You have that and then you have peoples' careers on the line."

"What about meeting with Eric Holder?"

"The Justice Department is going to allow the appeal to happen before anything else happens."

"What's the use of that if she ends up losing the appeal?"

He grinned. "Congressmen do not have legal authority under the United States Constitution to overturn the appeals verdict. The only person who could then give Dawn clemency is the president."

I looked at him in disbelief.

He laughed. "I have to tell you, in all the years that I've been involved in advocacy, this has been one of the most challenging situations I've had. It's a time where people are afraid to challenge their government. The people who you would think normally would not be afraid are afraid."

Ron Scott was born in Chicago and grew up in Detroit in the old Black Bottom area on the legendary Hastings Street. In the 1960s, when the civil rights movement was in full bloom, Ron Scott got involved. He marched with Dr. King, did community empowering work, and later became one of the co-founders of the Detroit branch of the Black Panther Party. As times got tough, Ron shifted gears and taught radio, television, film, and communication at the University of Michigan. But along the way, he never stopped being involved in activism. He worked on the 1971-73 anti-stress campaigns to stop robberies and make the streets safe, which led to Coleman A. Young becoming the first African American to be mayor of a major United States city. In the 1990s, Ron was asked to become part of an organization called Detroit Coalition of Police Brutality.

"Here I am, fourteen, fifteen years later," he'd said to me. "We've worked on over five hundred to six hundred cases. We've been to about three hundred funerals. We started talking about means for restorative justice in terms of finding ways to work out our conflicts together instead of just sending people to jail. I see the Dawn Hanna situation as reflective of that."

He paused, his white eyes so deep with meaning, it felt as if he was taking me a thousand years back to the world of his ancestry.

"We have to ask ourselves how we can transform our communities and rebuild them because our whole country is experiencing a devolution," he said. "We need to find a way to retain our rights as citizens, which is what the Dawn Hanna case is about. The First Amendment, the Fifth Amendment, the Fourteenth Amendment, the Eighth Amendment and so forth down the line. As human beings on this planet, in this particular time, we have major issues about whether any of us are going to survive. The question is, how do we work with each other to try to build peace so we don't kill each other?"

Ron Scott passed away at the age of 68 in November of 2015.

* * *

I was a little apprehensive about introducing Linda to Dawud after what happened with Issa, but I figured this guy was already hired by an organization to do advocacy work. Like me, he wouldn't be charging money, so what did we have to lose? We ended up meeting him at La Feast, a Middle Eastern restaurant located in the heart of Royal Oak.

"I met with Congressman Conyers last week," Dawud said, who I learned had previously served in the navy for four years. He was wearing an African matching pant set without the hat. "I didn't have enough time, as I would have liked, to thoroughly discuss with the Congressman Dawn's case."

The waitress brought a basket of hot bread from the oven.

He cleared his throat. "I entered the meeting with an attorney from a charity that had something to do with the Iraqi sanctions. They were providing food and medicine to the poor people during Saddam's regime. Anyway, the sanction issues took up most of the conversation."

The waitress returned to take our orders. I noticed a loud Middle Eastern soap opera playing in the background. Two of the waitresses had their eyes glued to the screen.

"There was still good that came from the meeting," Dawud said, taking bread from the basket. "I'm meeting in DC on Tuesday with Congressman Conyers as well as Congressman Hansen Clarke, and I will have exclusive access to one of the attorneys who is a staffer on the House Judiciary Committee for the minority. After that, I'm arranging for a meeting with all of the interested parties to speak with Congressman Conyers."

Someone screamed. It was a dramatic scene from the soap opera.

Dawud looked up only briefly, then continued. "To be frank, I will be there, but there needs to be someone more solid with the particulars of the case to lead the conversation. Besides a family representative, if we can get ACLU and ADC to join, that will be good. I had a passing conversation with ACLU-MI director as I was leaving the Federal Court today. I can follow up with her for the meeting, and getting Imad from ADC won't be hard. I'm not sure about how much more Joe Kassab from the Chaldean Federation can bring if he would even come. Weam may be good, though."

Darrin patted his hair and looked around. "I just feel like we keep repeating the same story over and over again," he finally said in an annoyed tone which I was not used to hearing from him. He seemed quite fed up, as if he would not have come to this meeting had his mother and sister not coaxed him into it. "Everyone from Washington knows this is a bullshit case, and yet no one can do anything about it. From before, we wanted Conyers to go to DC and meet with judiciary committee, but his office said, 'We can't get involved in active cases.' So when our senator watches people get prosecuted, he does what? Says, 'Oh well, this is the wrong branch. Can't touch it.' It's like you're calling Kmart and you call the wrong department."

"Ron Scott said that Conyers was really interested in helping," Linda said. "That he even wondered why there was hardly any media coverage for Dawn's case."

"Ron gave us over eighty of his media contacts," Darrin said.

"We freakin' called all of them and none of them would respond," Linda said.

"Of course not," Dawud said. "Major news channels are homogenized."

"There's a man in Washington who worked with counterintelligence for over thirty years," Darrin said. "He has been advocating for Dawn's release since the start, and he said that if the congressman wrote to the CIA, if he put pressure on them, the CIA people could end this with one call."

"I have a different take," Dawud said. "The CIA has

nothing to do with the direct prosecution of Dawn. Instead, we need to contact Eric Holder and have an international review of the case."

"We've been trying to get to him, but we can't!"

"If we can get enough organizational leaders who aren't chicken to ask congress to look into this case and have a press conference, we could make a difference."

Our dinner arrived.

"Linda, I want to let you know that I think Dawn is totally charming," Dawud said. He broke the thigh off the quail and ate it with his hand. "You and her father did a wonderful job guiding her mind and spirit."

Linda smiled, placing her fists near her stomach. "I was raised on good morals. My grandmother had a farm where I spent much time helping with the animals and crops, and my mother was head of the Royal Oak District for Muscular Dystrophy. She would take me along when she went to collect money. Being caregivers was a strong part of my family's work."

She was quiet, the chandelier light glistening on her face.

"We were encouraged to think for ourselves," she said, "and since eleventh grade in history class I could see we don't have democracy in this country. My daughter's case proves it. The other day I heard that the government is not happy that Emad came out. And they're upset that Dawn had a website up when she's in prison. I said, 'Excuse me! I have the website up. I bought the domain and programmed it.' But they were still upset and angry about it, and I thought, 'Well, so much for freedom of speech!'"

The waitress appeared, refilled our glasses with water,

and asked if we needed anything else. We told her no and Linda continued. "You know what makes me mad? Proctor from Channel 7 was so impressed with the story he told me he would try to have a half-hour documentary segment on it. That never happened. When we inquired for an update, Proctor did not even return our calls."

"I'm sure he was told not to air the story," Dawud said.

"By whom?" Linda asked.

"His higher ups."

"Yes, but who are these people who keep putting a door up and preventing the truth from coming out?"

"Television stations are visited by people in the government who approve or disapprove what will go on air," he said. "That has happened even with me, where they've actually told certain news channels that they can't interview me."

"Did Proctor say anything specifically to you about the case?"

"He said that he and his wife looked through every page of the court documents that he had access to. He had a bunch of footage sitting on his desk, but based on what he read and his conversation with Tom Cramner (Darrin's attorney), he thought it was best not to do a story. He said that given the sheer amount of communications that the government had of Dawn, it would not look good in her favor."

Darrin laughed sarcastically. "The other day a homeless man asked if I could spare some change so he can buy food. I said, 'I don't have change, but how about if I take you out to eat?' We went to a restaurant and spent a couple of hours talking about life."

Darrin's acts of kindness never failed to amaze me. A few

months ago his mother told me how once a week he invited his engineering students to his house for a dinner that he either bought or had her cook. He had lent one student money, and he had let another student live at his mother's house until he could afford to find his own place.

"I could have ignored this guy by rationalizing that his conduct let him become homeless, that he ought to get a job, that he shouldn't loiter our neighborhood. I could have manipulated my not wanting to help by shifting the blame on his homelessness. Right?"

"Yes, I agree," Dawud said.

"I mean, this is common sense! It doesn't need this spectacle!"

When we left the restaurant, the sun was still out. The weather had the perfect breeze for a nice stroll down Main Street. Linda asked if we could have coffee alone. I hesitantly agreed, since I had a limited time before returning home. We sat outside in one of the cafés and took in the lovely view of the shops and pedestrian traffic. My phone rang. It was Dawn.

"How did the meeting go?" she asked.

"It went okay, I guess. It's still all talk."

"What did you guys eat?"

"Are you serious?"

"Tell me!"

"I ordered chicken kabob. It was kind of spicy. Dawud ordered quail..."

"How did he fucking eat quail?"

"With his hands."

"What? Who does that at a meeting?"

"Dawn, you're seriously going to waste your minutes on what we ate and how we ate it?"

"Here I sit with a scoop of rotten tuna, expired and slimy lettuce, rancid tomatoes and dry wheat bread. How all of you could even eat in good conscience is a wonder to me, knowing I am stuck in here without freedom and clawing at the wheels of injustice to free myself. Shame on you all!"

"Shut the hell up. Now your mom and I are having a nice moment together, all alone without the kids, and you're spoiling it. So unless you have something important to say, goodbye!"

"I want to know what happened at the meeting!"

"News at 11!"

Linda and I burst out laughing and leaned against each other for support. We could hear Dawn cussing us out, which only made us laugh harder. After I hung up and she collected herself, Linda wiped tears from her eyes and handed me a bag which I thought she'd been carrying her files in. "This is a gift for you," she said.

"What for?"

"Just take it."

I opened the box. It was two flowery china coffee cups with matching square saucers. They were delicate and looked quite expensive. "They're too fancy to use," I said.

"No, use them!"

I kissed her on the cheek and gave her a warm hug. "Thank you, Linda."

"No, thank you," she said, pressing her tears onto my shoulders and releasing the emotions she'd buried beneath her smiles. The scent of her hair and perfume and the sound of her grief filled my heart, like gold, diamonds, and pearls spiraling in and around a jewelry box. "You have embraced us into your home like we're family," she said. "I'll never forget that."

CHAPTER 22
A Bodged Up Sentencing Guideline

The coffee cup Linda bought for me slipped from my soapy hands and bumped against the sink. I was relieved it did not break, but when I picked it up I noticed a chip inside, at the rim. I spun the cup in my hands, observing among the flowers two blue jays and a ladybug. I had not noticed them among the flowers before. Blue jays are talkative creatures that vocalize their opinions. Their speech abilities are so advanced, they are able to mimic other birds and even humans. Ladybugs caution people not to try too hard or go too fast to fulfill our dreams, to let things flow at their natural pace.

The sight of the chipped rim bothered me, but I forced myself to set it aside and begin preparing a lunch of curry stew with steamed rice. A rerun episode of *The New Jersey Housewives* kept me entertained as I sliced and marinated potatoes with curry and vinegar and simmered the chicken with garlic and onions.

Linda called. "The appellate judges returned with a decision!"

Her voice was shaking. I couldn't tell if it was in a good or bad way.

"I saw at the top of the list USA versus Dawn Hanna and I froze. I can't open it."

Linda subscribed to the Sixth Circuit Court Appellate decisions. She received opinions every day and glanced over them, hoping she'd one day see Dawn's name. I told Linda I would be right over. Then I hung up and called my sister. "Something important just came up and I have to leave the house immediately," I said, pulling out a pair of jeans from the closet.

"What's wrong?" She was very worried. Unless it was an emergency, I never demanded for someone to watch my kids on a whim.

"The judges came back with a decision!"

"What judges? What decision?"

"For Dawn's case!"

"Oh, wow, she's getting out?"

"Yes, I think so." I was going to fall trying to get dressed while talking on the phone and untangling my son's arms from my calves. "Just come over quick."

When she came over, I asked her if I smelled like curry.

"I can't tell," she said. "The whole house smells of it."

I added another spray of perfume, grabbed my camera, and rushed outside. It was a beautiful warm Friday in August. The early afternoon sun was good enough to get a tan in. Before I got into my car, I remembered something and retreated. "The stew is ready. Can you just steam the rice?"

My sister stood against the open door, smiling wide. My kids were beside her, blankets and sippy cups in hand, staring at me with a confused look on their faces. "Drive carefully and don't forget my *hallawa*," she said.

In the Middle Eastern culture, if one participates in a good deed that has a positive outcome, they get *hallawa*. The *hallawa* could be anything, from sweets to jewelry.

The drive to Linda's workplace was a good twenty minutes. The radio was on and the traffic on Rochester Road was plump, but I heard and saw nothing aside from the images in my head of Dawn reuniting with her family. I imagined her eating dolma, pacha, and barbecue in the house her stepdad Rick expanded from 800 square feet to 2800 square feet in order to accommodate his new family, the house where he and her mother had a December wedding. They had had 125 guests and four cats, all crammed inside to escape the cold. The cats were kept in the bedroom, but during the ceremony, one of them came out and meowed all over the place. Everything went well except that by nighttime, they couldn't find Darrin. Linda went berserk, thinking they'd lost him. They looked all over for Darrin and found him asleep on two chairs, still in his tuxedo, with a table cover over him.

The ranch-style home is in a quiet neighborhood and sits on a small hill. Whenever our car went up the long driveway, Linda's two mini dachshunds, Lucy and Katie, appeared from behind the screen door and barked their hearts out. "Lucy, Katie, come inside," we'd hear Linda shout as I'd try to unbuckle my son out of the car seat. Her nephew, in his early teens, was often there on the weekends, helping her with housework or the landscape. He absolutely loved his aunt and spent at least every other weekend at her house. Once he'd wanted to see her so badly that when his mother told him she couldn't drive him to Linda's house, he got on his bike and rode for some ten miles to get there.

Last winter, I had invited Linda to stay at my house when her heat broke. She politely declined and instead turned on the fireplace every day, spending the majority of the cold nights wrapped up in heaves of blankets and cuddled next to her dogs. She preferred doing that than burdening her son by asking for money, as he was still paying his legal fees. And she definitely didn't want to deduct from the $320 monthly allowance she sent Dawn in order to fix the heat, nor did she want to discontinue sending hygiene gifts to a few inmates in Dawn's prison, who, during Christmas, had no one to remember them. There was a young girl whose mother, an inmate, could not afford to buy her anything, so Linda made a basket of soaps and shampoos and snuck in a twenty dollar bill in a Christmas card and happily mailed the package out to her. She did the same thing on the girl's birthday.

The heater was not the only problem in the house. A part of the ceiling in the living room caved in at one point, and whenever it rained water dripped inside. The last time we were at Linda's house, I saw a large piece of silver electric tape over the area. I asked her if that helped the leak. "No," she said. "I don't know. I just put it there for…" She couldn't find the word, laughed, and said, "Decoration."

I passed the Barnes & Noble on Rochester Road, the same one where I'd driven the women of my family to pluck fresh grape leaves from the back of the building; where Dawn and I once hung out, separately; where I met Linda for the first time. I reminisced over the friendship that Linda and I had developed. From the start, Louie suggested that Linda visit my home to busy herself with something outside of Dawn's case, so I invited her over for coffee. Little by little, our coffees turned into elaborate dinners where we drank wine and vented about personal issues. She split her attention between me and the kids, who sat on each side of her lap on a rocking chair she'd brought from her home. We laughed at ourselves or at others, like when my son took off his diaper and ran across the house naked with me trying to track him down, or when Bonnie called periodically, informing me she was having yet another meeting with the prime minister of Iraq, and did I have a last request?

I arrived at Linda's work and rushed to the second story of the building without taking the elevator. When I entered the office, Barb, the receptionist who was also Linda's friend and a strong advocate of Dawn, was calm and collected. "Hello," she said.

She was so composed that my excitement began to fizzle. Linda came out to greet me. She was nice and smiling, but there was no excitement. "Darrin is in the other room," she said. "You can go in and talk to him."

"What's going on?" I asked.

She shook her head. "It's very confusing. He'll explain it to you."

I went into a room on the left corner. Darrin was sitting behind a desk wearing a red, short sleeved shirt. He was on the phone with Dawn. "Who called you?" he asked her. "Deday called you? He emailed you?"

Darrin acknowledged me, and I sat down on a chair across from him. There was typing sounds coming from the other rooms, heard clearly between the tension in the air and Darrin's long pauses as he listened to Dawn.

"But what does that mean?" he said. "Well, what did the email say? There's a lot of details to that. Why don't you call him and see…what, what, what, the whole what?"

In the end, Darrin decided he would call Deday.

"Well, just wait, Dawn. One step at a time. I don't know. Let me talk to Deday and find out exactly what's going on." He coughed. "What? I think so. Just sit tight. Sit tight. Let me see if I can get a hold of Deday. Yeah, yeah. Just wait. Yeah, Dawn. One step at a time. Just wait." Long pause. "Let's not overreact to anything. Let's sort things out and figure out what's what. I mean, we don't know anything. We just found this out from you." He paused. "It's horrible."

He hung up the phone and immediately fumbled inside his pockets for some business cards. "She got an email from Deday saying we lost the appeal."

He called Deday. As Deday explained the situation on the other line, Darrin made sketches with a red pen on a piece of paper. I sat in a daze, taken back to that eerie feeling that we once had living under Saddam's regime: the fear, the inability to fight back or to do anything about a wrongdoing. All the noise we had made for Dawn's case did nothing. I wondered if "freedom of speech" was just a permission to nag, given by a witty husband who allows his wife to nag to her hearts' content without him doing anything to change the situation.

After Darrin hung up, he explained some of what he understood from Dawn's attorney. "The appellate court said that the sentencing thing was all wrong," he said. "The sentencing guideline should have been done under something called Section 1701, which would have resulted in a significantly lower sentencing range because there would not have been the national security enhancement. The reason they did not overturn it in the appeal is because Deday, during the trial sentencing, argued for 1705, and the Judge gave him what he argued. It's called an induced error, which if you argued it, even though it's an error, you can't argue the other way on appeal."

This was very confusing to me. I remember when I read the court transcripts. The communication between the Judge and Dawn's attorney in regards to figuring out her sentencing was baffling. It made no sense. They went back and forth and back and forth trying to figure out where Dawn's crime fit into the Guidelines Appendix. At one point the Judge even said, "There's some other guidelines if you go guideline shopping, but we can't do that."

Deday was very adamant about the inappropriateness of the Judge adding national security enhancement to Dawn's sentencing, but the Judge added it on, stating to Dawn, "Even though the government agrees that you did not intend any terrorist activities or to do anything against your country or to support another country to do it, I think this is probably the thing that has bothered me the most about your case, and that is, when you listen to the facts and you listen to the discussion that came out here in the arguments, that word terrorism seems to overtake everything…"

So she added the national security enhancement, but it turned out that no other case involving an embargo violation in any circuit had charged a defendant under the guidelines she'd used. All were merely charged with an export violation.

"Deday said it was an error," Darrin said. "Appellate court agreed it's an error, but because Deday argued on behalf of that error, he can't now argue to reverse that error. He's making an appointment with Barbara McQuade for next week. Basically, he's going to go and tell her, 'Look, this was a complex sentencing and it's costing Dawn time and I feel very badly.' He's going to try to see if she's willing to correct it."

I turned off the camera. "You know, Darrin, in my birth country, knowing that they were oppressed, people risked their lives digging for the truth and found it. Here, our leaders sedate people with the idea that we are better than any other country in the world. This larger-than-life belief makes a person too lazy to want to find out the truth for themselves and play a stronger role in their own destiny. And it makes it so easy for the government to justify their unjust decisions – like wars, sanctions, imprisonment – with a formal written document."

"What a great way to oppress someone than to make them think they're not oppressed," Darrin said.

I walked out of the room, feeling empty. Smiling nervously, Linda greeted me as if she was a hostess at a party. She took me into the conference room, where she had carryout Chinese food waiting for me.

"I'm not hungry," I said.

"You must eat something before you go back home." She sat down and I sat across from her, glaring at the colorful food that would have, under different circumstances, looked appetizing. "The appellate decided that the new CIA information would not be helpful to the defense," she said.

More specifically, they concluded, "*The information might have been interesting for a jury to hear, but a prosecutor's duty is not so broad as to require him to disclose any information that might affect the jury's verdict.*"

"It is apparent that power and position rank over justice," Linda said as I stared at her suffering.

On the way home, I talked on the phone with Fred, the man in Washington who was just as shocked by the court's decision as I was. "Everything they claim is secondary to the big picture," he said.

"Yes, but what does that matter?" I asked. "They can do whatever they want."

The appellate judges, who described the error as "far from harmless" also concluded, in the same document, that the district court did not abuse its discretion when it considered *ex parte, in camera* pleadings filed by the government pursuant to CIPA, adding,

> "Even if this court were to conclude that the district court erroneously applied the national security enhancement, the district court's sentence should still be affirmed. This is because an improperly calculated Guideline range does not require a remand and resentencing if the error was harmless."

Five months after Dawn lost the appeal, on January

2012, Thomas W. Cranmer, who represented Darrin during the first trial, submitted a brief to vacate Dawn's sentence since the Sixth Circuit Court of Appeals had considered that the court had committed a "far from harmless" error. Along with the brief was an affidavit from her attorney, Deday, stating that he acknowledged that he had failed to provide Ms. Hanna the level of representation that she was constitutionally entitled to receive in connection with her sentencing. The brief stated:

> Ms. Hanna is not seeking to walk away unpunished. She asks only that she be required to serve a period of imprisonment that appropriately reflects the mistakes that she made and not a sentence that is infected by the errors of the attorney who undoubtedly did his best to represent her, but ultimately played the key role in delivering many more years of punishment than she deserved. For these reasons, Ms. Hanna respectfully requests that her sentence be vacated and that the court set this matter for resentencing as soon as reasonably practicable.

Dawn sent me an email that read, *"Did you read the Affidavits that Deday submitted to the court on this latest Motion? Please get a copy of both of them and show them to the fucker attorney who had said to you, 'Dawn must be guilty if Deday couldn't get her off.'"*

She was talking about an attorney in our community

who discussed Dawn's case with me. Eating his bagel at Panera Bread, he shook his head and said, "Dawn must be guilty if Deday couldn't get her off."

There was no reply from the court until Monday, June 11, 2011, at 11:30 am. Linda received an email from Cranmer informing her that Judge Battani had denied their motion to vacate Dawn's sentence. She found that Deday's sentencing advocacy was not ineffective because it was "motivated by strategy." She also determined that there was no prejudice caused by the erroneous guidelines calculation because she imposed a sentence that she felt, and still feels, was appropriate under the circumstances.

At 4:23 pm that day, I received an email from Linda.

My dearest Weam,

It is with an extremely heavy heart that I write this email. Just as my heart sank this morning as I read the subject line of this email, it has taken this long to regain my composure, being at work, and to write you. I didn't bother reading the motion. I am so very, very disappointed and disgusted with our entire judicial system. This negative decision brings to mind when Fred was informed to "back down" along with others who, with knowledge of this case, said it was a set up.

Excuse my language, but who in the hell has such power behind this case and a tight hold on keeping my daughter in prison! Who, at what level in our government, considers themselves God? While I have much respect for those who have served, are currently serving, our country, and condolences for those families of the many who have lost their lives in war, I think I can safely say, "I hate this country."

Love,
Linda

When Emad learned of the news, he wrote, "I am sorry that you are still struggling for justice in the land of the free. I think you would have obtained better justice from Saddam Hussein."

CHAPTER 23
Double Standards

Eight months after Judge Battani had denied the motion to vacate Dawn's sentence, the *Los Angeles Times* reported that the Los Angeles County Sheriff's Department had committed criminal export violations over ten years ago when it funneled hundreds of bulletproof vests, without a license, to Cambodia through the City of Gardena, California. Federal investigators decided not to press charges on the grounds that there was no evidence that anyone involved in the transactions were aware of the relevant export laws.

The double standards between the people and the government not only continues, but the gap has been made bigger as the government more aggressively cracks down on activists, prosecutes whistleblowers, and prosecutes and spies on journalist with the usage of the Espionage Act.

"For the powerful, crimes are those that others commit," wrote Noam Chomsky in *Imperial Ambitions: Conversations on the Post-9/11 World.* He was also quoted to have said, "It's not radical Islam that worries the US. It is independence."

In September 2007, the same month that the trial started, Darrin's company, TIGS, and Shelby Township sued each other shortly after they signed a contract. The township terminated the contract when they learned that Darrin and his sister were indicted by the US Attorney's Office for violating financial embargo with Iraq. In 2009, a Macomb County jury ruled in favor of the township, ordering a monetary award from TIGS. In March 2013, the Appeals Court reversed this verdict and ordered judgement in favor of TIGS in the amount of $450,000, the amount value of two years of a three-year contract their company had with the township, not counting the legal fees and interest that could be tacked on.

"The evidence indicates that township officials decided to back out of the contract because they perceived the Hannas as unsavory individuals with connection to terrorism," said the three-judge appeals panel. One of the judges had even told jurors to ignore references such as "9/11," "terrorist acts," "rifles," "memorial for soldiers" and "foreign-sounding names" posted on a board because they were irrelevant.

I'm not a mathematician, but I imagine that the cost of this circus – the investigation, plus the trial, plus the imprisonment, then the lawsuit – could have been used in many other more beneficial ways to make us safer, healthier, and wiser.

Dawn was released from prison in 2014 and chose to lead a private life. Emad and I had a few more conversations about Iraq and politics. I once told him I heard a rumor that the houses in Iraq were being bought at huge prices, paid in cash, by Jews so that they could make Iraq their land since so much of their history lives there. He said, "Iraqi Jews have strong ties in Iraq. Daniel, the guy in the Den of Lion's biblical story, is buried in Iraq. Ezra is buried in Iraq. In the Hebrew Bible, Ezra returned from the Babylonian exile and reintroduced the Torah in Jerusalem. The Jews have been in Iraq since Babylonian time. Iraq and the Jewish are very interlinked. They are part of Iraq's tapestry. If some of them come back and buy in Iraq, well, why not? If the Iraqis were wise, they would allow the Jewish to come back to Iraq. I know a lot of Iraqi Jews and they are the kindest people."

He told me about a Jewish Iraqi who owned a restaurant in London. He never went after customers who gave him bounced checks, figuring if they couldn't afford a good meal, he was more than happy to provide them with one.

"Not long ago, the Jews, Christians, and Muslims lived there in harmony," Emad said.

"Yes, that's what I've heard and read," I said, remembering *My Father's Paradise* by Ariel Sabar, a Kurdish Jew whose family still spoke Aramaic. I fantasize about such a day returning because of what my daughter once said to me. "Momma, I want to one day visit Iraq."

"Why, Momma?" I asked.

"Because I want to sleep on the roof."

"Who told you about the roof?"

"You did."

I smiled. "One day, baby, when the situation there is better."

And one day, I prayed, it will be better, here, there, and everywhere.

As a little girl living in Baghdad, my younger brother and I heard stories about America that made us think that America was a most magical place. My sister, seven years our senior, would sit us down and tell us how in America, each person owned and rode a horse. I guess cowboy movies were very popular in Iraq.

"In America, one never runs out of eggs," she said. "Eggs are so plenty, people boil them by the dozens and play games with them where one person holds a hard-boiled egg and taps the egg of another person with his own egg, trying to break the other without breaking his own. They even crack eggs on each other's heads."

I am not sure whether she saw this on *The Three Stooges*, but my younger brother and I were in awe, especially since eggs were a rare commodity, available to purchase in the *souk*, and only God and Saddam knew when. It was not that Iraq had a shortage of eggs, or milk, or bananas, or tomatoes, or sugar, or chicken, or beef or whatever else was hard to find in the market. This was simply the Iraqi government's way of keeping its people "busy," or as Americans would say, "oppressed."

It did not take long for me and other Iraqi immigrants to see that our new government, like the one we previously lived under, had its own ways of keeping its people "busy" and made them "busier" every day. I noticed through the Dawn Hanna case that the American people had given their power away to the government and were having a hell of a time getting it back. Those who did not even see their blind

surrender were like the boys and girls who mistook infatuation for love. Infatuation slips you into a fairytale that dom-
inates you, makes you totally available for a rule's beckon
call. If the rule summons you away from your family to wear
some gear and go into a battlefield to kill or be killed, you feel
a rush and excitement and romantically oblige.

Love, on the other hand, allows you to look at the reality
of what you love so that you can know it for what it really is
rather than what it looks like from the outside.

"In any relationship, if you are only giving or only receiving, then there is an imbalance," my Native American teacher
once said to me. "That's when the essence of the relationship
is no longer about love, but about control."

My mother never went to school or worked outside
the house, but she knew a lot about marriage. Not just the
conventional type of marriage, but one between relatives,
communities, and a people and their government. The majority of people would agree that equal marriages mean that
neither husband nor wife seek to dominate the other. Yet in
many countries, including the United States, the rules of an
equal marriage do not apply to the relationship one has with
their government.

Blind love is not promoted in any culture, and a statement like this spoken by President John F. Kennedy, who
I am sure meant well when he said it, actually takes power away from an individual: "My fellow Americans, ask not
what your country can do for you, ask what you can do for
your country." Imagine if these words were used as wedding
vows: "My darling wife, ask not what I can do for you, ask
what you can do for me."

Then one day, I learned that a Jewish man running for presidency wanted to create an equal marriage by encouraging us to serve each other so that there would be a healthy balance between the government and its people. Perhaps one day America will resemble the type of marriage that already exists in many parts of the world, which once upon a time, thousands of years ago, existed in the region that today is called Iraq.

The End

The Great American Family documentary is currently in post-production. To view the trailer or for more information about this case and why it matters, visit the website:

www.thegreatamericanfamilydocumentary.com

OTHER BOOKS BY HERMIZ PUBLISHING, INC.

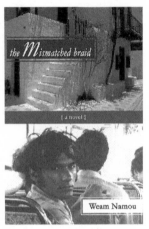

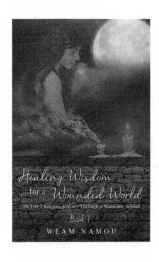

The Feminine Art
(ISBN-13: 978-0975295625)
A novel about a married woman who distracts herself from
boredom by trying to find her nephew a wife

The Mismatched Braid
(ISBN-13: 978-0975295632)
A novel about an Iraqi refugee living in Athens who falls in
love with his American cousin

The Flavor of Cultures
(ISBN-13: 978-0975295663)
A novel about a Chaldean girl in America who tries to find
her individuality while maintaining her tribal lifestyle

I Am a Mute Iraqi with a Voice
(ISBN-13: 978-0975295694)
A collection of 76 poems

Healing Wisdom for a Wounded World
My Life-Changing Journey Through a Shamanic School
(Book 1)
(ISBN 978-0977679041)
Namou's memoir about her apprenticeship in a 4-year
shamanic school that is founded and run by bestselling
author and mystic Lynn Andrews

Iraqi Americans: The War Generation
(ISBN-13: 978-0977679096)
A collection of 36 articles that Namou wrote over the years
which paint a picture of Iraqi Americans' political and
social situation and their struggles

Iraqi Americans: Witnessing a Genocide
(ISBN-13: 978-0977679072)
A nonfiction book that provides the Iraqi American view on
Iraq and the Islamic State

Iraqi Americans: The Lives of the Artists
(ISBN-13: 978-0977679010)
A book about the rich lives of 16 artists who are of
Mesopotamian descent

26611229R00176

Made in the USA
Columbia, SC
17 September 2018